MW01290707

The Burden and Blessing of Memory

In 1941-'44, I was under Nazi occupation and faced imminent death. We, who lived, promised ourselves that if any one of us would survive, we would tell the world what the beastly Nazis did to us, and not let the world forget. Soon, survivors will no longer be able to give firsthand witness. For future generations our stories must be easy to read and understood. My story has a happy ending and there are many lessons to learn from it.

ANN JAFFE

ISBN: 9-781387-577729

Library of Congress Control Number: 2022912365

Cover design and book layout by Jaidy Schweers.

All images courtesy of the Jaffe family.

Printed by Lulu, Inc., in the United States of America.

First printing edition 2022

For media inquiries or permission requests, email losjov@gmail.com

Dedication

To my beloved children (Rebecca, Linda, and David).
To my cherished grandchildren
(Maayan, Tali, Joshua, and Rachel),
my adored great-grandchildren (Caleb and Eden),
and to the bright future of my family.

Contents

Timeline

1926 - 1935 Josef Pilsudski was Premier of Poland.

1927 David Swirski and Chava Gordon are married.

1931 Ann is born. She is their third child.

1935 - 1939 After Pilsudski's death, antisemitic Rydz-Smigly ruled for four years.

1939 Poland is divided between Nazi Germany and the Soviet Union.

1939 - 1941 Jews lived peacefully under Soviet rule.

June 12, 1941 Sheldon is born (10 days before the war begins).

June 22, 1941 Nazi Germany attacked the Soviet Union beginning WWII.

September 21, 1942 The final solution to kill all the Jews in Kobylnik. (Yom Kippur)

1942 - 1944 Twenty months surviving in the forest.

July 4, 1944 Liberation. Those that were hiding were allowed to return to their homes.

1946 Meyer reunites with the family after almost four years apart.

May 11, 1948 The State of Israel is born, while we are in the DP camps.

1951 The family takes transatlantic ship to Halifax, Canada.

July 4, 1954 Ann marries Ed Jaffe in Toronto, Canada.

1954 One month later, David Swirski dies of a massive heart attack in Toronto.

1957 Rebecca is born in Brooklyn, NY.

1960 Family moves to Union, New Jersey and Linda is born.

1964 David is born.

1975 Family moves from New Jersey to Wilmington, Delaware.

1977 Ann speaks publicly about her experience for the very first time.

1982 Chava Swirski dies after having a stroke two years earlier.

1994 Ann returns to Koblynik (Naroch), for the first time since the war.

2020 Delaware legislates the teaching of the Holocaust in public schools.

2021 Ann is inducted into the Delaware Women's Hall of Fame.

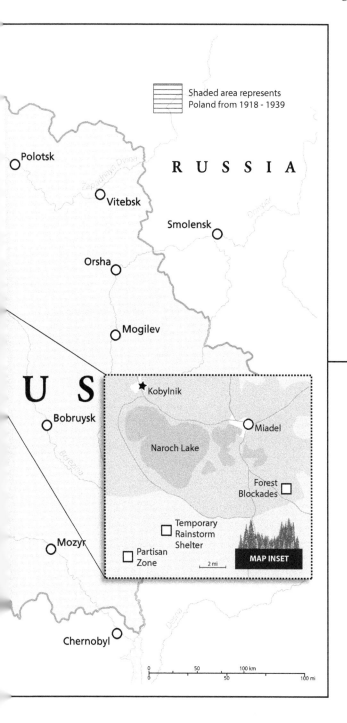

Shaded area represents
Poland from 1918 - 1939

Polotsk

R U S S I A

Vitebsk

Smolensk

Orsha

Mogilev

U   S

Kobylnik

Bobruysk

Miadel

Naroch Lake

Forest
Blockades

Temporary
Rainstorm
Shelter

Mozyr

Partisan
Zone

2 mi

MAP INSET

Chernobyl

0   50   100 km
0   50   100 mi

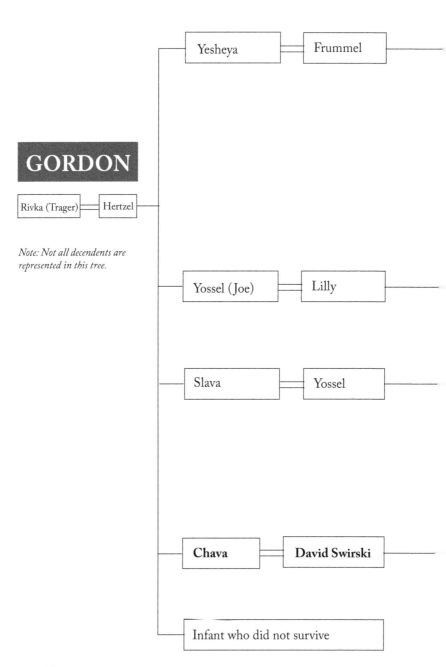

Yesheya — Frummel

GORDON

Rivka (Trager) — Hertzel

Note: Not all decendents are represented in this tree.

Yossel (Joe) — Lilly

Slava — Yossel

Chava — **David Swirski**

Infant who did not survive

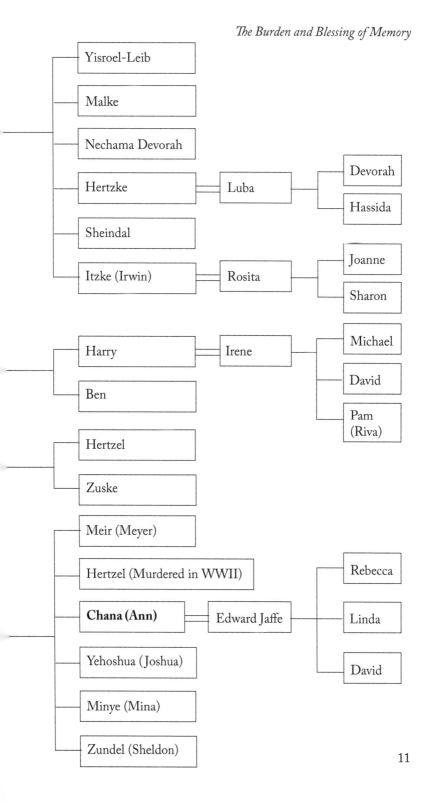

Yisroel-Leib

Malke

Nechama Devorah

Hertzke — Luba — Devorah
— Hassida

Sheindal

Itzke (Irwin) — Rosita — Joanne
— Sharon

Harry — Irene — Michael
— David
Ben — Pam (Riva)

Hertzel

Zuske

Meir (Meyer)

Hertzel (Murdered in WWII) — Rebecca

Chana (Ann) — Edward Jaffe — Linda

Yehoshua (Joshua) — David

Minye (Mina)

Zundel (Sheldon)

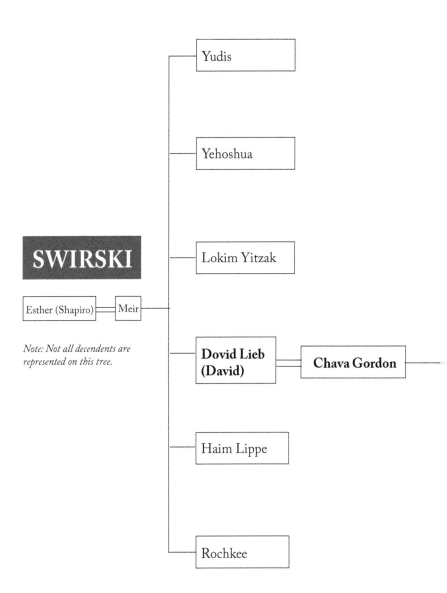

SWIRSKI

Esther (Shapiro) — Meir

Yudis

Yehoshua

Lokim Yitzak

Dovid Lieb (David) — Chava Gordon

Haim Lippe

Rochkee

Note: Not all decendents are represented on this tree.

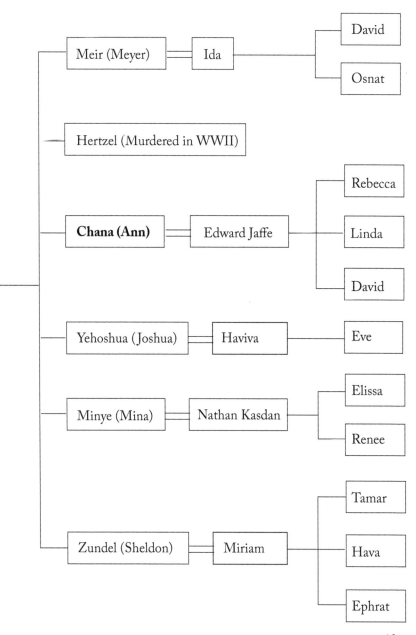

Preface

I have been asked by a great many people to write down my story. Speaking publicly about my war experience for almost half my life prompted these requests. Some of the memories are so painful to relive I have avoided this task with great determination. What follows is a sparing, firsthand description of my survival. Many details are missing because it is simply too agonizing to describe each event and all the accompanying feelings.

I was born in 1931. We used Jewish dates to mark significant events in our home. My mother described to me the time of my birth as "one week before *Rosh Chodesh Adar.*" *Adar* is a Jewish month, and *Rosh Chodesh* is the beginning of it. I was the third child born to Chava and David Swirski, but the first daughter. I am 91 years old and have only one sibling still alive with me now. Although we reflect back continuously, I live my life with a fervor and purpose that only some can understand, and even fewer can fully appreciate. There are all kinds of survivors in this world, and I admire them all. Some of us have survived the worst you can imagine. At times it was a living hell, but with my family, as a Jewish child, I survived WWII in Eastern Europe, and live to tell my story.

At birth, I was named Chana. Here, in the United States, it wasn't easy for people to pronounce my name correctly, because it begins with a sound not found in English. (Clearing one's throat is something like it.) When we came to this country, we were eager to assimilate, so it was not a difficult decision to change my name. I chose Ann. I like it plain and simple, with no "e." My maiden name was Swirski, which means "belonging to the lake of Svir,"—a body of water close to my birthplace. Many of the families that lived near that lake took this family name. It was a typical Polish name, which was also used by a few Jewish families.

If you come across people with a similar name, I would bet that at least one of their ancestors lived close to the lake of Svir. Once we emigrated, some of my family chose to spell our family name with an "i" at the end, and others with the "y." Later still, when I married, I changed my last name to that of my husband. That is how I became Ann Jaffe.

Of course, who I am has little to do with my name. I was born to wonderful parents with strong religious beliefs and rich Jewish cultural traditions, in a small town in Eastern Poland.

1

Remembering the Beginning

When a worm makes his home in a horseradish,
he thinks it's the best place in the world.

—An Old Country Saying

This is how I remember my childhood. The little town of Kobylnik, in eastern Poland was my horseradish. It is not in Poland any longer; it is now in Belarus. In fact, our town no longer lives on a modern map. Sometime in the mid-1960s Kobylnik became Naroch (also known as Narach), named for the substantially larger lake located approximately three kilometers from town. The only place you will find the old name is on the tombstones.

The only reason it qualified as a town was because of the presence of a police station, a fire station, an administrative office, and a schoolhouse that progressed to the eighth grade. The administrative office also served as the Post Office, where one could find the only telephone in the entire town. If you needed to make a phone call or receive one, you had to reserve the phone in advance.

We had no running water or electricity. Almost every household had a well and an outhouse. No one had a car. The mode of transportation was horse and buggy. Once a day a bus came through our town that stopped and continued to Vilna. The smell of gasoline from the exhaust was such a novelty to us that many kids, including me, ran after the bus to smell the engine emissions.

The total population in my youth was about 1,200 and it was almost evenly divided between Poles, Belarusians, and Jews. The Polish Catholic church dated several hundred years back. The only time I saw the inside was during a funeral or wedding, when the Jews were asked to sit on a back bench; hardly any Jewish adults stepped into the church.

The Belarusians were almost all Russian Orthodox, and from the outside, their church was the prettiest. I had never been inside the Russian Orthodox Church. I only knew that their leader was called "Father."

The Jewish people prayed in a synagogue. It was a very small wooden building set out of the way, with a small living quarter attached in the back for the Rabbi and his wife.

The Jews numbered about 350 in my day (making possible the acquaintance of each and every one), and they decreased rapidly trying to get out of Poland any way they could because of the rampant antisemitism. Things were bearable under the leadership of Jozef Pilsudski, but when he died in 1935 everything changed. His successor, Edward Rydz-Smigly, was a great admirer of Hitler and he instituted many anti-Jewish laws. At the same time, young Poles organized in what was called the "Nationalists," who made life in Poland for the Jews very difficult. They would stand in front of the Jewish stores and scream, "Don't buy from Jews," or they would shout, "Jews go to Palestine; we don't want you here." However, inside our home the atmosphere was entirely different. The warmth and love shared by my parents and maternal grandmother made us feel happy and secure.

Many generations of Jews had lived in this area. Despite the feeling of home, most would have chosen to emigrate to Palestine, but that territory was under British rule, and the quota to enter was very small, open mostly to the young and skilled. That said, I do know that about a half a dozen young people from Kobylnik settled in Palestine and were considered Pioneers of the resettled land. Some people went to South Africa. Our neighbor's son, then a young man, went to South Africa and wrote back that there he found a good place for Jews to settle. Others went to the Soviet Union (before we understood what the Soviets were all about). All the intellectuals, poets, and writers who went to Russia were later killed by Stalin. That is why America became the preferred destination, but again the quota for Eastern European Jews was small and very few could afford the price of a ticket. The outside world was hostile and dangerous, but inside our home there was love and tranquility.

2

Kobylnik

Most of the homes in Kobylnik were made of notched wooden logs, although there were several brick homes owned by wealthy families. When fires became a problem, many of the thatched roofs were replaced with large sheet metal shingles. On our block, there were several houses that sat on a lower plane on either side of the elevated road that traversed our town. Our house had six or seven descending cement steps that led to the doorway. My father had them put in when a cement worker was in town working on a different project. We had suffered one too many falls on rainy days, so he felt it was important. As kids, we usually ran down the hill, leaving the steps for our grandmother, parents, and other older people. Those steps distinguished our home from all the rest and were the only sign of that childhood home that remained when I returned 50 years later.

Our town was a little more than one mile from a big lake. On some hot Saturday afternoons my whole family would walk there. We children usually ran ahead, jumping and dancing with joy, or dragged behind, searching for natural treasures, while mother and father walked arm in arm at a steady pace. My parents would not allow swimming on the Sabbath, but we were allowed to take off our shoes and dip our feet in the lake, enjoying the cool breeze off the water.

My parents had a beautiful story, well before they started our family. My mother was born in this same little *shtetl* of Kobylnik, something we had in common. My father's family arrived to Kobylnik when he was three years old. He was born in Hodutishki (Adutishki), a nearby township. As a second daughter, my mother, Chava, had to wait for her older sister, Slava, to marry first. Slava was a pleasant girl, but unfortunately, she did not catch the eye of a gentleman for quite a while. At first this was not distressing, but as my mother's lengthy courtship blossomed, poor Chava and David were forced to wait it out.

3

A Meaningful Courtship

Before World War I, Kobylnik was referred to as a village because it was smaller than the days I remember as a child. That is where my parents' courtship took place. The Germans had occupied that area in their attempt to conquer Russia around the time of World War I, and stayed in Kobylnik for quite a while, using up all the provisions our farmers could deliver. As a result of this occupation the town's people suffered terrible hunger. The only people who had food to eat were those employed by the army. Even if one had money, there was no food to be bought.

My mother's family was among those who were hungry. They would go days without food. My father's family, on the other hand, had enough to eat because he worked as an interpreter for the German army. Father was the fourth of six children. He was intelligent and talented. By the time the Germans arrived, he already spoke and wrote in four languages: Yiddish, Russian, Hebrew, and Polish. Since Yiddish is similar to German, he was also able to learn German quickly and became an interpreter for the German army, for which he was paid well.

My mother was the youngest of four children. Once her three older siblings graduated from the local school around the age of 10, they were each sent away to learn a trade as an apprentice. Her oldest brother, Yesheya, left home first to become a tailor. Yossel (Joe) apprenticed as a carpenter, and Slava became an accomplished seamstress. Chava was the only child who remained home with her mother and did what she could to help. My grandmother, Rivka, actually had five children but the last one died in infancy. That baby was born only days after Rivka's husband died suddenly. Grandmother was left to care for the mortgaged home and children all alone and fell into a state of shock. It was rumored that this last baby might have died from neglect.

At that time of the German occupation of Kobylnik, my father, David, was summoned to translate for a German officer in their acquired headquarters. On the way there he noticed Chava throwing out dirty water from a bucket into the street gutter near her home.

Eager to communicate with her, he approached and said, "I am glad to see that you are not suffering from hunger. Someone with red cheeks like yours probably has enough to eat."

Exhausted and hungry, my mother looked up into his eyes and tears began to well up. "My cheeks are red because I just finished washing the floors on my hands and knees. I haven't had a bite of food for two days. What do you know about hunger?"

Having made her cry David felt badly. He apologized for not realizing her situation and excused himself. Later that day he returned to Chava's home with a loaf of bread. He handed her the bread and asked for permission to come back the next day. This is how the courtship started and continued for ten years, far longer than they had hoped.

Matchmaking was not overt, but families did try and guide their children in matters of matrimony. My parents were in love at a time when many marriages were arranged with a dowry—wealth on the woman's side to make the match. My mother's family had very little to offer because her father died young and left her mother (my grandmother Rivka), to raise her children alone.

In a small village like Kobylnik, Chava and David already knew of each other before that chance meeting. At the time their relationship started, they were ages 17 and 19, respectively.

David was being groomed to marry someone from a wealthier family because he was educated, but having met Chava and gotten to know her, he was drawn to her. It appeared there was no changing his mind. Chava did not have the pedigree his family hoped for, but David fell for her nonetheless. Though thin, she was beautiful. In those days being thin was less attractive as it was a sign of poverty as well as having too much hard work. Chava had a round face and thick, jet-black hair that was pulled back neatly. She was dedicated to her family, hard-working, and modest. As they became more familiar, David also realized that she was very witty and smart. David came by her house regularly just to sit on the front stoop to see her and chat. In a poor little village, this was the equivalent of dating. They both came from religious homes, so touching was taboo. Mother claimed it took three whole years before David even dared touch her hand. As the years passed, they became very familiar with one another, but always in a manner of respect.

My mother was not formally educated like my father, but she knew how to read and write in Yiddish and Russian. She was also very smart and had an incredible work ethic. However, the things my father appreciated most about her were her wit, her piety, and her kindness.

He would come by every evening to sit with her outside where everyone could see them for the sake of modesty (following Orthodox Jewish custom). He read the newspaper to her and discussed the news of the day.

By small town standards, my father was not only well educated but also handsome. For that reason, many matchmakers approached him with lucrative possibilities. These were daughters of wealthy businessmen who could provide large dowries. My father didn't even want to meet them.

Rivka noticed Chava was growing attached to David, so she asked to speak with him privately in her front living room. She expressed concern that he might be leading Chava on, as he could surely find a more fitting match. But David assured Rivka that his intentions were noble and serious. When Slava and Chava overheard this through the wall, they both began to cry, but took care not to be heard.

David's mother was not happy about his resistance to a better financial match. She was an assertive woman and must have given my father a hard time. My parents' courtship continued with no end in sight as mother's older sister Slava had still not found a match. Slava was an excellent seamstress and could have easily provided for a family, but she had no dowry. As it turned out, my father had an older unmarried sister too, which added to their wait. Ultimately, both women procured dowries from extended family in the United States from my mother's brother, Uncle Joe Gordon, and my father's brother, Uncle Herman Swirsky, who each sent $100 to make their match.

With a change in season and a new harvest from their garden, hunger became a distant memory for a long time. By then, my mother's red cheeks faded though she remained skinny because of the hard physical work.

Because she was so thin, people in their village were overheard saying "Chava must have consumption."

My father responded: "As soon as we will get married, I will plant an orchard around our property and Chava will be the first to taste its fruit!"

When my parents finally did get married, after both their older sisters wed, my father was 29 years old, and my mother was 27. At that time this was considered late in life. My mother's dowry was the family house and the piece of land on which it stood, with the understanding that my grandmother would live with them.

They married in the closest big city of Vilnius (Vilna), with only close members of their family present. David's parents were not in attendance, because they were ill. It was the beginning of 1927 and exactly nine months later their first son was born. They named him Meyer, after my paternal grandfather who passed away a few months earlier. By naming a new child after a deceased relative, the family perpetuated their loving memory. This continues to be a custom among Eastern European Jews and many of their descendants.

My siblings and I witnessed our parent's love affair continue throughout their lives. They were excellent role models in every way. In fact, it was my father who ultimately changed my mind about the world we live in, and how to make a difference in the lives that I would touch. When they finally did marry, so totally and thoroughly in love, my mother later told us, "Courtship is like a closed telegram. Not until after the wedding are the contents opened and realized."

4

Our House

I remember my childhood home very well. Like most of the houses, it was made of wood logs with a metal roof. There was no indoor plumbing, though after World War I the Germans installed electricity and ran it to most Kobylnik buildings. As it turned out, this new electricity was putting the small-town kerosene wholesaler out of business, so the wholesaler hired a few thugs to cut the lines to each house and it was never repaired. When I picture the house, I do recall a cord dropping from the ceiling, but it remained disconnected. We lit the rooms with kerosene lamps that hung from the ceiling. Our home had wood floors painted rustic red. Only the kitchen had a packed dirt floor, which we kept clean. We were never considered poor because we always had food to eat. But each of us had little more than a change or two of clothes. In lieu of store-bought toys we created fun by exploring nature, and sometimes made our own toys from what we found. Life was not particularly easy (especially for my mother), but before the war we created a happy way to live in Kobylnik.

Our home was a single-story duplex that my mother's father (my grandfather), Hertzel, bought in the late 1800s from the town's Christian landlord, who had owned all the town's property at that time. Originally it was one large home. When my grandfather died, it was left to his wife, my grandmother Rivka. Shortly thereafter, the house was modified into two separate homes, so that she could rent out one side for income. A Rabbi rented it out for quite a while, and my mother, as a young girl, often spent time on that side of the house because she liked learning about Judaism. That Rabbi told grandmother that Chava would be a pious woman one day. Eventually, when mother's eldest brother, Yesheya, got married and had a family, the Rabbi was given notice to leave, and their family moved into the second side. Grandmother lived with us in that house until her dying day. That house sat on a large plot of land, with a small barn in the rear yard, where we kept our one cow, flock of chickens, and two horses—which belonged to my uncle. On occasion our cow would yield a calf, which was raised as food for the long winter. We also had a covered water well on our property. It looked like a kid's house with a small roof and a windowlike hole in the roof where we would crank a handle to pull up the bucket of water.

The front door led to a small unheated foyer with a high window allowing sunlight to brighten our kitchen wall, directly behind it. Our side of the duplex was slightly larger than the other, and even as a child I understood that was because grandmother lived with us. Any way you measured, both sides were small for the number of children who lived there. Our door was to the left and opened into the largest room, which was our dining room. It had one large wooden table, flanked by two long benches. This room had a brick wood-burning oven built into the center wall to heat the house. It had a doorway which led to the left, facing the front of the house. Through that doorway was our living room. In the far-right corner of that room was mother's sewing machine, along with a small couch that sometimes doubled as a bed. Guests were entertained there.

To the right of the central dining room was a small kitchen that was immediately behind the unheated foyer. The packed dirt floor was as clean as dirt could be; with the splashing of water, mother always did the best she could. The most prominent thing in that kitchen was a large brick wood-burning oven that had a large exhaust chimney that fed through the roof. Brick stoves were sometimes covered with plaster and were built with insets on either side of the fire hole for wood storage, and space below where some families kept their vulnerable chickens during the coldest time of winter. On the backside of the chimney, parallel to the fire hole, was a long plateau extension that felt like a separate room because the height and width of the chimney divided the space. Although difficult to envision, this rear oven extension was often the first spot guests would choose to sleep, especially in the winter because the plaster was warm from the stove on the other side. With no indoor plumbing, the kitchen had only a large bucket to wash food and dishes, with a separate trough, where we poured out dirty water and vegetables scraps. Someone would later remove it and take it to the barn to water and feed the animals. The kitchen table was used only for preparing food. We ate in the dining room. In a separate corner of the kitchen was a pail of clean water, with a copper cup that we used to drink or wash our hands. In the far-left corner of that kitchen there was an open-faced cabinet where mother stored spices, all her dishes and cookware. Most of our food was stored in the unheated storage room at the very back of the house where wooden barrels held cabbage picked from our garden. That room was a walk-in refrigerator. The shelves of a simple wooden armoire held pickling jars with sour cabbage, fresh fruits and vegetables, and any other food mother cooked that we would eat weekly.

Behind the living room were two rooms. My parents slept farthest back in a room with a window and door. The larger interior room was divided by a large armoire, so it felt like two small rooms. My sister, Mina, and I shared a bed closest to my parents (in the middle); and my brothers Meyer, Hertzel, and Joshua shared the bed closest to the living room. We had two out-houses (one for each family), but each person had a chamber pot to avoid leaving the house at night. When Sheldon was born, he slept in my parents' room in a cradle. Grandmother had the smallest room just off the kitchen. I can still remember her bed (where each of her grandchildren often asked to sleep with her), and a second much smaller stove where a metal bucket warmed water for her to wash clothes. The unheated room behind the house stored everything else, in addition to food.

Mother's oldest brother, my uncle Yesheya, and his family lived on the other side of the duplex, which was a little smaller in size, but his half had a large below-ground cellar, where both families stored out-of-season dried fruit and vegetables.

We bathed outside of our home. Our custom was to go with mother to a community bathhouse once a week. She paid to use it. This building was a separate structure that was one large room. In the corner was a stove with an exhaust pipe. Burning wood heated a large pile of stones on the stove and a large bucket of clean water could be found two feet away. Part of the value of the bathhouse was the warm hot steam that hung in the room because water was being dripped onto the hot stones. Mother would carefully use a tool to place a hot stone in the bucket of water and within moments we had warm water to wash ourselves. Of course, we used the water sparingly, and mother helped us wash starting with the youngest child, and she used the dirtier water lastly for herself. Father bathed separately.

We lived our lives under a blanket of care and concern, which was always present in our home. The warmth and love shared by my parents and maternal grandmother made us feel happy and secure in our modest surroundings.

5

Childhood Memories

Ever since I can remember, Grandma insisted that we come out and help her with the gardening. Adjacent to our house was a large piece of land. We made it into our vegetable garden, and grew enough vegetables (cabbage, beets, onions, carrots, and potatoes) that lasted us almost the entire winter. Potatoes were our staple food eaten every day and was the only crop we needed to supplement through purchase at the market. I was always happy to spend time with my grandmother. She made a real good gardener out of me. To this day, when I go out into my garden, I think of Grandmother with continuous joy and fondness.

The sweetest memories of my childhood were the outings with my grandmother to the forest. Since we had no electricity, my grandmother went to bed as soon as it became dark. She would announce to all the children, "Anyone who wants to come with me to collect berries and mushrooms better be ready at sunrise." I always wanted to go with her. The reason for starting out early was to gather the best mushrooms; these would pop up overnight, especially after a good rain, before anyone else picked them. Everyone was welcome to join, so long as we obeyed Grandmother's rules. Grandmother always wore a long skirt and a large full-length apron over it. Each gathering participant was given a tin cup for the berries, but if we found mushrooms, we were instructed to place them gently into Grandmother's apron, which she lifted by the corners to create a soft carrying space. She also had a woven basket and when we filled our individual cups with the berries, we would empty them into Grandma's basket.

When noontime came, the basket was usually full, and we would sit down on a nearby toppled tree trunk and eat our lunch. Grandma took out a few slices of home-baked bread; she gave everyone a piece, which we ate with delight, along with the last cup of berries we had picked that morning.

When we arrived home, we were welcomed warmly by our mother. The mushrooms were sorted by categories. The fragile yellow ones (*Lishitzki, Chanterelle*) were cooked right away and made into a delicious and fragrant mushroom potato soup. The sturdy ones with the brown caps (*Baraviki, Portobello*) were carefully cleaned and then strung onto twine and hung out to dry for the winter. It was one of the staples that sustained us all winter long. The berries were made into sweet jams and were a special treat served with hot tea during long winter nights. These are the gratifying memories of my childhood before the war.

* * *

Even as young children, we felt antisemitism hanging in the air. Sometimes there was clear evidence to remind us of this fact. When Meyer, my oldest brother, was of age he was sent to public school. Jewish children did not attend religious lessons at this school and were asked to keep busy outside during that time. One very rainy day Meyer asked if he could sit in the back of the class during the lesson and just listen while staying dry. The way he described it, he believed his presence in the room might have prompted the teacher to overemphasize that Jesus was killed by the Jews.

Meyer raised his hand and asked, "Wasn't Jesus Jewish?"

The teacher responded "Yes . . . they killed one of their own!"

This incident caused a big scandal and Meyer was expelled from school. Father had to meet with the administrators of the school to plead on his behalf, but ultimately paid them off under the table to allow his return.

The church also taught that Jesus was crucified by the Jews. When Christian kids wanted to bully us Jewish kids, they would throw rocks at us and scream "Christ killers!" My cousin, Hertzke, would never put up with kids taunting him, least of all because he was a Jew. He built himself a sturdy wooden briefcase for his schoolbooks, and if kids approached him with mischief in their eyes, he did not hesitate to swing that wooden case as hard as he could right at their heads. When he did, they ran away like scared animals, and Hertzke had a good laugh. Hertzke offered to walk Meyer to and from school (with the wooden case in hand) as protection, but only if he paid Hertzke the equivalent of a few pennies for each trip. He was a budding entrepreneur.

I also believe that envy played a part in the hatred. Jewish families were artisans and businessmen living comfortably. On the other hand, most of the Christian population were farmers that just got by.

* * *

When I was seven years old, my father took me to visit his sister and her daughter in a town 12 kilometers from Kobylnik. He rode his bike and I sat on the crossbar for the entire trip. Father traveled this way almost every week to bring extra money to his sister (the one that married before him); her husband turned out to be a useless spouse who didn't hold a job and made no money. She went door to door in her town to secure any work she could, even for a small amount of change. She would clean, kneed bread, and carry firewood. On the occasion when I joined my dad, he gave her the usual donation to buy food for the Sabbath. In turn his sister suggested that I stay overnight to play with her daughter; father could return to pick me up the next morning. And so, I did. The next morning my aunt prepared one egg (which is all she had), cutting it in half for me and her daughter. The daughter began to rant that she wanted her full egg, and the suggestion of sharing with a visiting relative fell on deaf ears. I was so embarrassed because eggs were plentiful in our home. I pushed my half of the egg to her side of the table and said, "I don't want the egg! I have my own eggs at home." Even today, when I eat an egg, I think of that incident. A great many of the village folk were poor and miserable even before the war. Although my father gave money to his mother and sisters regularly, we didn't suffer too much because my mother was so very good with the money we had. Relatively, we were quite comfortable.

* * *

Our specific family had a few things that almost nobody else had. This was probably because both my parents worked and made money. They also both had a sibling living in the

United States that gave them access to some items others could only dream of in a remote town like Kobylnik. For example, my father's brother regularly sent him a Yiddish newspaper printed in the United States. After father was done reading the newspaper, it would circulate among all his neighbors. It was in that newspaper that he read about a fishing net made of nylon. Father was a wholesale fish merchant. He had partnered with a villager who owned a boat. That fisherman brought my father his catch of the day, and father would sell it wholesale to other merchants for the retail market. Whatever profit father made on the sale, he split with the fisherman. Initially that fisherman worked with a twine net, but on occasion the fish bit through the rope and swam away. He could mend it, but news of the nylon net changed the outcome. Father asked his brother, Herman, to ship him a nylon fishing net; when he received it, he gave it to his fisherman friend. The quantity of fish caught increased substantially. Father packed the fish with extra ice and took them to larger cities where he sold them at an agreed upon price. The profit was split 50-50, and everyone benefited.

There was also an incident of sale in a larger city, when the buyer reneged on the agreed upon price for the fish. My father couldn't walk away because the fish, on melting ice, would spoil—timing was everything. Father agreed to take the lesser price for the lot. When my father was about to leave town, he recounted the money and realized the buyer made a mistake in Father's favor. He returned to the buyer and gave back the difference. The buyer was stunned at his honesty. He said, "Swirski, whenever you have fish to sell, I will never turn you down and promise to always give you a fair price." Word spread of my father's honesty, and for that reason, among others, he made a good living, enough to support his mother's medical bills and help his sisters with money almost every week. Father's reputation also helped us in the forest. That fisherman helped with food as much as he could, and during times of destitute my father's good business relationships usually helped us.

6

The War Begins

News often arrived late to our remote little town. My parents both read newspapers when they were available, though reading alone did not make reports of escalation feel real. I believe they knew that WWII was beginning to take hold of the world. I remember that one of our relatives from Adutishki was sent to the war front without any military training and never came back.

We sensed that Poland would not be able to withstand the mechanized German army. It was not a question of *if*, but *when* the Germans would arrive. In 1939, to our great surprise, instead of the Germans, the Russians marched into our town, quickly announcing equality for everyone. We were temporarily relieved. Although this was an unwanted change, it was much preferred to the Germans. The two years under the Soviet occupation were good years for us children. The adults understood things differently. My father was given a government job managing the distribution of single-shot rifles to hunters, who later brought back animal furs. The income this job provided gave us some peace of mind.

As a child I was not upset the Russians shuttered the Jewish school. We kids were happy to go to a public school and hoped that the name-calling and shaming was over because the Russians proclaimed us as equals. We were happier to be in a school mainstreamed with everyone. In this school they didn't teach religion. However, children like me, were forced to repeat some grades because we didn't know any Russian. I repeated the second and the third grade. We learned Russian quickly because it is very similar to the Belorussian language, which we heard spoken constantly.

The Russian rule brought new leaders, new authority, and new language almost overnight. As difficult as that sounds, we accepted the change without panic because we sensed far worse might be near. The Russians tolerated the very old people attending church or synagogue, but when they saw younger adults like my parents try to attend, they would chase them away and warn them not to return. Generally, we were able to maintain some customary lifestyle. As a rule, the Russians didn't like rich people and we were not among them, so we had two peaceful years between 1939 and 1941.

* * *

For my family the war started on June 22, 1941, when Nazi Germany, led by Adolf Hitler, attacked the Soviet Union. My baby brother, Sheldon, was born ten days earlier (June 12, 1941), and I was ten years old.

Only a few days later, German planes dropped a bomb directly on our marketplace. There was tremendous panic. The Jewish refugees that had escaped from Western Poland and settled in our town told us to run for our lives. There had been only one German family (*Volkdeutch*) in our town that had remained after WWI. Seeking answers, my father met that man in our destroyed marketplace and asked him how the pilot knew where to drop the bombs? Calmly this man invited my father to his basement and showed him the apparatus with which he transmitted this information to the Germans. "After all, they are my people." That German man disappeared from the village that same day.

We had heard about how the Nazi regime treated Jews. We believed that much of it was an exaggeration, but having our town bombed brought the reality of the war to our doorstep. Our town was completely rural. There were almost no cars, buses, or rail transportation. As we thought of trying to escape, we were faced with the challenging fact that we were a family with five young children and a newborn infant.

Because of the general location of our town, we had only one major road paved with cobblestones, that led to much bigger cities like Polotzk to the north, Vilna to the south, and then forked off to Minsk further southeast. As soon as the war erupted, this main thoroughfare was jammed with cars, trucks, civilians, and the military trying to escape to Russia. People were so desperate to leave that when a truck drove by, we could see it was filled to capacity and more people were standing or hanging onto any part of the vehicle they could grab. The Russian defense collapsed quickly and completely. They didn't even have enough military trucks to retreat into Russia. The front-line soldiers were running on foot wearing torn boots and clearly exhausted. The hysterical commotion and loss of everything we held dear made it feel like the end of our world.

A few of the young Jewish men who had bicycles tried to escape into Russia. Even my father considered using his bike to escape.

He reasoned with my mother, "The Germans will probably not harm women and children so it will be best for our family if I disappear with the bicycle."

She looked him square in the eyes realizing immediately that as head of the household he was particularly vulnerable and said, "Of course. Try to get away."

This must have been an agonizing moment for both my parents. My mother was left with six young children ranging in age from a few weeks old to 14 years old. She also cared for her mother. With abject grief, Father got on that bicycle and tried to ride away into Russia. Before he could even reach the next big town, the German army was there, stopping people. He jumped off the bike and tried to appear as though he was there on a routine errand. He tried to remain unseen. It was a desperate act, because how far could a man get on a bicycle? Father heard that the Germans had already occupied the next town. Authorities were checking everyone's identity and travel papers, and nobody was permitted to simply leave. Father had to sneak back into our town so people wouldn't know that he had tried to escape. Had they known, he would have been one of their first victims. With fear, we heard a Jewish neighbor mutter below her breath, "We didn't know your husband was a communist. Why else would he want to run to Russia?"

During the ten days prior to the Germans' actual arrival in our town, many of the local Christian population organized a pogrom (preparation to rob and kill the Jews). They appeared happy to greet the Nazis. We were helpless with nobody to defend us. My father ran to the priest with whom he was friendly (because they played chess together on occasion) and asked him to intervene.

His response was, "Tell me Mr. Swirski, what will I tell my parishioners when they ask me why I am defending the Christ killers?"

My father came home and said, "The situation is hopeless." In that ten-day period, we tried to bribe the locals with whatever we had to temporarily halt any action against us.

When the mighty German army marched through our town, it sent shivers down our spines. Following the German army, we saw the Russian prisoners of war. How could our Russian protectors fail? Now, as prisoners, many of them had no shoes; their mouths were parched from thirst and hunger. We watched from afar and wept. We wanted to throw them a piece of bread or hand them some water, but the guards pulled out their guns to show us that it was forbidden, and they meant business. My heartbroken father mumbled, "If they can do this to prisoners of war, imagine how they will treat us." When they arrived at our town, any chance of escape was long gone.

The *Wermacht* (German armed forces) left to oversee a larger territory and did not establish a garrison in our small town. Only two regular German soldiers were left behind to look after the telephone line. We sensed that they were not hostile. When some of the local hooligans started to break windows in Jewish homes in order to extort goods from us, we turned to the two German soldiers for help. They told us that they were not allowed to mix into local affairs. However, when they saw the hooligans out in the streets, they would put on their impressive army hats and pretend to go for a stroll. The hooligans disappeared and never came back. Ironically, in this case, the Germans protected us. All of this happened in the first few weeks of the occupation.

Instead of a garrison, a few *gendarmes* (German officers) from a neighboring town showed up and asked our Christian neighbors to form a volunteer militia in Kobylnik. There was no shortage of young men who volunteered to help the Nazis, which was very painful to us, as they were not strangers but our neighbors. We grew up in this small town together. My older cousins went to school with them. We had celebrated public holidays together, but given the chance, they chose to collaborate with the Nazis and became our executioners. The hatred from our neighbors (now militia) was clear, present, and astonishing. It left us questioning: How could they possibly hate us so much? We never did anything to harm them yet given the opportunity they appeared to follow the Nazi orders gladly.

We didn't realize the depth of hatred toward the Jews, but we knew it was taught to them in schools, churches, and at home. That same day, *gendarmes* hung up announcements in the marketplace pertaining to all the people of Kobylnik: one side for Christian people and the other side for Jews.

For the Christian people it was very simple:

WE CAME TO LIBERATE YOU FROM COMMUNISM. IF YOU FOLLOW OUR RULES, NOTHING BAD WILL HAPPEN TO YOU. HELPING OR SHELTERING JEWS IS FORBIDDEN. ANYONE WHO DARES TO DO SO WILL BE PUNISHED LIKE A JEW.

For the Jews:

1) ALL YOUR CIVIL RIGHTS ARE ABROGATED.

2) JEWS MUST NOT BE OUTSIDE AFTER DARK.

3) EVERY JEWISH PERSON MUST WEAR A YELLOW STAR ON THE FRONT AND BACK OF THEIR OUTER GARMENT. (*Small babies are exempt.*)

4) EVERY JEWISH HOME MUST HAVE A JEWISH STAR PAINTED ON THE FRONT OF THE HOUSE.

5) Every able-bodied person must report for work.

6) Everything made of gold, silver, or any other metal must be turned in immediately.

7) Fur coats and warm boots must be turned over to the German authorities.

I remember feeling shame as my mother sewed a yellow star on my coat, but she tried to comfort me by saying, "It is best we all have the same star." The panic among the Jews became palpable. Decisions had to be made about what to turn in and what to hide. My parents gave away their wedding bands, our candlesticks, and my father's fur coat. Everyone contributed something. Some of my parents' nicer clothing was given away to our Christian friends for safekeeping. We had to also turn in our bicycle and the cow, which was our only source of milk.

My mother's cousin was a single woman who had 500 rubles saved as a dowry. Because my father had the finest reputation as an honest man, she gave my father the rubles just before all properties were confiscated to hold for her in the event she would survive. My father took some jewelry of their own and buried it with the 500 rubles in the basement of our home.

By now the *Gendarmes* from the neighboring town showed up more often, always with new orders, demanding gold, and other specified items. If we didn't follow their orders they threatened us, saying they will kill several Jews in retaliation for our disobedience. All of the Jews in our town were in a literal panic, and as children we could only hide in the corners of the house and try to be invisible. At the end of the day, when the Nazi officers left, we felt a touch of relief.

We were scared for our lives because the killing started very soon after the Nazi occupation. The local militia took control of the police station. German authorities chose a *Burgemeister* (Mayor) who was a well-known anti-Semite. He was not born in our town but married a woman from Kobylnik and made his home there. The *Burgemeister* gave an order to kill all known communists; he and the local militia selected four Jews and some Christians. We realized that these few people were somehow connected with the Russian occupation in our area. One was a schoolteacher, and another a barber who openly praised the Soviets for liberating us and giving everyone equal rights. All of them were labeled communists.

Our local militia was not satisfied with just killing these people; they first tortured them for 24 hours, let them go home for one day, and then rearrested them. Some of them were not able to walk to their execution and needed to be carried before they were shot. We had to pay ransom to the militia in order to bury the four Jews in our Jewish cemetery. The panic, fear and helplessness affected all of us, especially the adults. We all understood that the first killings were to ignite fear in us. This first execution gave us a taste of what was to come. If these people could be labeled and picked randomly for execution, we knew we could be next.

The children also felt danger acutely. The barber who had just been killed had only one son, who was my friend. He was always kind to me and came to play with us because we had a house full of children. After his father was killed, one day he came over to our house and told me, "I don't know what to do or where to hide. They say that the families of the first victims will be killed next. I wish I could find a hiding place." Even as a child I understood his situation, but there was nothing I could do. Though I wanted very much to help him, we could not hide him in our house because non-family members were not allowed to be found there, or we would all be killed. I knew he was right; the rumor had also reached us. I didn't know what to say. I felt very sad to say goodbye to him.

We quickly devised a way to hide Father in a crawl space in the attic, under some wooden crates out of sight. Later we realized other families did the same thing. We understood that when the head of a household was taken away for certain death, it was only a matter of time before the wife and children were also rounded up.

My cousin Shainke was assigned to clean the police station latrine. Shainke was 16 years old and very pretty. Fearing she would be harassed or raped, her parents asked my parents to send me in her place because I was only 11 years old and drew significantly less attention. Because I now had a job to do, I was allowed to walk outside and my dog, Mooshka, followed me. At this time Jews were no longer allowed on the sidewalks. From time-to-time Mooshka would move freely onto the sidewalk and then back to the street; my dog had more freedom than I did.

If Christian neighbors had any kind of grievance against a Jew, they could easily go to one of the local volunteer militias and complain with fabricated lies that a person was "no good," or "that one is a communist." They especially singled out our rabbi, who was quite old, and his son-in-law, who was also a rabbi. They were dragged into the militia station and beaten. Because these men were considered our scholars, it was an extra layer of humiliation. The local militia did it purposely—to laugh and jeer at us.

As German soldiers were being transported to the front lines, they stopped in our town for a rest. One day one of these soldiers suddenly walked into our house. We were startled by his unannounced entry and scared for our lives.

My father addressed him respectfully: "Didn't you see the Jewish star on our house? We are Jews."

"That is the reason why I came in," he said. "We know what the Nazis are doing to the Jews. They don't care about ANY of us. I am nothing but a sacrificial pawn to them. Our *Fuhrer* doesn't care if my wife will be widowed, and my children orphaned. Hitler says he wants *lebensraum* (living space) for his people. I don't need *lebensraum*."

He tugged at his shirt with anger and continued, "I am not proud to wear this uniform. Your chances of survival are greater than mine! Keep a low profile and try to hide somewhere. Hitler will not last forever."

Not all Germans were horrible Nazis. Even though many of them felt forced to join the military, they were not all glad to inflict harm. Some were also trapped in a bad situation. My father thanked him.

Under the Nazi occupation food was always scarce. Father and Meyer were taken out daily to do hard labor along with other strong men from the town. They were sent to the roads edge to cut down trees and split wood. Our forest was so dense, the Germans were afraid that Partisans might go unnoticed into the woods. Clearing those trees was an attempt to avoid that, supply firewood, and allow some light to penetrate the woods. When they returned from a full day of work, each laborer was given a cup of soup and a slice of bread. Father and Meyer shared the bread with the whole family, but we insisted that they drink the soup. We had to barter with Gentiles for food, with whatever we still had (clothing, furniture, and other small hidden trinkets). Toward the end of the 15 months, when everything was taken from us, there was a time that we completely ran out of food. Our lives were wrought with anxiety and hunger. Even so, Mother tried to make something out of nothing. She found one head of cabbage somewhere in the shadows of the cellar and made cabbage soup for the family. My siblings and I sat at the large dining table when mother brought in the soup.

She handed me a bowl of cabbage soup and said, "Eat it."

I never liked cabbage soup and replied, "No, I am not hungry."

She said, "I know you do not like it, but it is the only thing we will have to eat today, so I want you to eat it."

I was defiant and said "No, I am not going to eat it."

In that moment, my otherwise soft-spoken mother slapped my face. That was the only time she ever hit me, and she was instantly sorry.

She took a quick breath and with anguish in her voice said, "Go and look in the cupboard and the storage places and even in the cellar. There is *nothing* else left but this one head of cabbage. There will be no other food today!"

I began to cry and reached out for her. She quickly embraced me, and we cried together. She knew I didn't like the soup, but it was all we had. We tried to comfort one another: mother and daughter, under these horrible circumstances. I still cannot remember whether I ate the soup or not, but I have a feeling I did.

7

The Second Killing

A second cousin of mine, Michel Patashnik, escaped from his nearby town and came to tell us how all the Jews were murdered as soon as the Nazis arrived there. They were rounded up from his town and several other places and taken to a place called *Poligon*, on the outskirts of yet another town. Earlier, Michel's two younger brothers had escaped that massacre and found their way to Kobylnik seeking refuge with our family. But when they saw how small and rural our town was, they realized quickly they would easily be noticed and decided to move on to Postavey, approximately 28 kilometers from our town. We already heard from some Christian farmers that 10,000 Jews were killed by the Lithuanians. Now we had to hide Michel to make sure nobody saw him. If he would be discovered, all of us would have been shot.

When Michel was hiding in our house, it brought back memories of the two summers I spent in his town. Before the war, one of the Patashnik daughters came to us for a visit. She saw that my mother had her hands full with five children and asked if she could take me to her town (25 kilometers away) for the summer. I was delighted and we did this two summers in a row. I had a wonderful time there. One of her daughters and I slept in the loft on straw mattresses. That second summer, while I was there, the Nazis attacked Poland, beginning WWII. My mother promptly came to get me and take me home. It was Patashnik's son who was mobilized for the Polish army and never came back.

Up until that time, we had not yet experienced the kind of mass killing that Michel described. A few months had passed since the first group of Jewish individuals was killed in Kobylnik. But when you kill indiscriminately, it does not take genius to target the wealthy first. This is exactly what they did. They simply rounded up all the members of the wealthiest families, marched them away, and killed them. We were lucky not to fall into this category.

All the belongings of these 54 murdered Jewish souls were taken from their homes and put into a warehouse. Christians were permitted to take whatever they wanted. We suspected that the militia wanted their property, and this was the easiest way to get it; take them away and kill them.

The executioners had the victims first take off their shoes, coats, and then everything else except their underwear. They were instructed to kneel and were then shot in the back of their heads. Hearing this, the young rabbi called out to the Jews in the group, "Don't kneel! We Jews are not allowed to kneel. Lower yourself to your hands squatting," and he did so when it was his turn. Everyone saw this as an act of defiance and devotion.

This second larger massacre devastated us all. We learned details of it from firsthand eyewitnesses who were chosen to dig the large grave and then cover it up. Entire families of men, women and babies, young and old were taken. Among them was our Rabbi's son-in-law with his wife and baby. This one family consisted of grandparents, their daughter, husband, two girls and an infant boy. Before the war I used to play with their young girls.

Their execution epitomizes the savage cruelty that took place. The grandfather asked to be shot first so that he would not have to witness the execution of his family. The Nazi officer did the opposite. He was put aside and ordered to watch as each execution was carried out. His daughter, who held the infant in her arms, begged the German executioner to spare the baby's life. Screaming and crying, she said, "He is innocent. Why should he be killed?" The Nazi officer grabbed the baby by the legs, hit his head against a tree and threw him into the pit. This unimaginable cruelty is still impossible to forget.

There were a few more people I remember who were victims in this massacre: my mother's cousin, who was my grandmother's niece, as well as her husband and two children. The girl was about eight years old and the boy an infant. More about them a little later.

The barber's son and wife were also in this group. He wanted desperately to hide but didn't know where. The people who covered up the grave told us that the bullet they used on the barber's wife did not kill her immediately. They had no choice but to bury her when she was still alive. It broke my heart.

One day towards dusk, so no one would see him, the rabbi appeared at our back door and reassured us that no one saw him. He was completely black and blue and begged us to let him in. He knew we still had some ice in our shed and hoped maybe my mother could put some ice on his wounds. He told us his beating was done by militia men just for fun.

My mother tended to his wounds with ice compresses and begged him to go home to sleep and never mention he was in our house. After he left, my father told my mother in earnest that he would go to the pharmacist the next day and try and purchase poison. The pharmacist told him he had no poison, not even for himself. This incident made me think about what happened to the pharmacist and his family. He had come to work in Kobylnik and was considered the wealthiest Jew in town. I do not remember seeing him at the last execution.

It turned out that he found a farmer who agreed to hide him for pay. The druggist's family was hiding in the attic loft of the farmer's barn. His daughter, who was exceptionally beautiful, found out about the partisans in the forest and decided to leave their hiding place and join those freedom fighters. It was not uncommon for the partisan group leader of each unit to pick out the most beautiful woman in his unit to be his "war wife." When the partisan leader asked the druggist's daughter to accept this role, she refused. Insulted, he sent her on a mission and made sure she would not come back alive. Toward the end of the war, we learned she was killed by orders of her commanding officer.

The fate of the pharmacist, his wife, and his son, we learned much later, when we were already in the forest. That farmer realized that the druggist kept his money on him, and he decided to kill him and take the money. He managed to murder the pharmacist, but the wife and son escaped into the forest. Unfortunately, during the next blockade, they were both caught and killed. I think of this family often because I always admired them, and thought if anyone might survive, they would. Almost a year later when we were hiding in a different forest, we found out they did not.

The fact that the richest pharmacist family in Kobylnik could not survive the war, makes my family's survival extraordinary. This surely contributes to my single focus on family. It has always meant a great deal to me, and the fact that all three of my children ultimately settled within 30 miles of me, is perhaps not a coincidence. Eventually they all learned my story and the lessons my father shared about hate. Each of my children and grandchildren are fine people who care deeply about those they know. It is a lesson that keeps on giving to all of those who employ it.

* * *

A day or two after tending to our battered rabbi, a Christian woman—who knew my mother well—walked into our home unannounced and asked my mother if she would be willing to give her our baby boy. She explained to my mother that her daughter couldn't have children and she would be grateful if we gave her my baby brother. Under any other circumstance this would be unthinkable. Since she came by after the second massacre, it was a tempting offer because our situation was desperate. My mother told her that a decision like this required her husband's approval. The woman answered back, "What is there to ask? They will kill you all anyway." My mother also realized that in an effort to save my baby brother by giving him to this woman's daughter, the woman would likely complain about us to the militia, and we would be the next victims. Despite that realization, Mother decided not to give up my brother Sheldon, who was about 10 months old at that time. "We will either live together or die together. It is in G-d's hands."

All of this was an absolute nightmare, as the fear of death was unrelenting and there was no escape. All children of a certain age were instantly transformed into adults.

We knew our chances of surviving were extremely small. It seemed that the feeble old people and young children really didn't have a chance.

My 20-year-old first cousin, Yisroel Leib, wanted to run and hide and posed this idea to his parents. His mother said, "If you can live with the fact that your escape will cause the death of other family members and friends, then go." He paced the room, with his head down, rubbing his head, and pacing some more. We were all holding our breath, waiting for him to decide. His nervous energy seemed to push him to the far wall of the house. With his back to the wall, his knees began to bend toward his chest as he slowly slid down to the ground in a ball of defeat. He did not run. We felt like trapped animals, scared of our shadow, and sick to think of every new day.

Even after Yisroel Leib had been persuaded not to run, we were sure that other young and strong men struggled with the same decision as my cousin. Because Kobylnik was not a closed ghetto, one could run. But even if you did, where could you go? The Christian people were often eager to turn you in to the local militia. Even if you found a Christian person who was kind enough and willing to help, the new law was clear; if Christians helped hide a Jew, they would be caught and immediately killed. Not only that, their family and house would be burned to the ground to send a message that helping Jews would not be tolerated. We thought there were others who wanted to help us but under these circumstances, it was unrealistic to think that people would willingly endanger not only their own lives, but more importantly, the lives of their families.

When a random count of heads revealed a missing person, the militia announced, "If you cannot produce the missing person within 24 hours, we will take hostages and execute them immediately." We were panic stricken since this quickly did happen. They did give us 24 hours, but despite our fruitless search, they grabbed people at random, running into houses to see who was there. The people (five fathers) were taken away for execution. We were inconsolable.

A few days after her father had been taken away as a hostage, my personal friend from school, and another girl who lived two houses up the street, along with their mothers and a sister, were taken and marched in front of our house to the cemetery. I was sick with sorrow and desperation. Shaking uncontrollably, I thought to myself, "Why doesn't she run away? Why is she just marching to her death?" For a second, I thought I saw her turn her head to look for me in our house window, but I was frozen with confusion and helplessness. They were shot on the grounds of the Jewish cemetery.

Militia men would get drunk regularly and let firsthand stories reach us. That is how I learned that when it was my girlfriend's turn to be shot, she was ordered to face away from the gunman. She answered him, "Are you a coward that you cannot shoot me to my face?" A second later she was dead. The cumulative effect of these executions left us riddled with constant fear and absolute hopelessness.

Two months after the mass execution the Jewish community was given permission to transfer our murdered brethren to the Jewish cemetery after first bribing our militia with whatever we still had. Among the people who went to uncover the graves and prepare the corpses for a ritual burial was my grandmother Rivka. When she saw her niece (mentioned earlier) holding the baby boy in her arms in the execution pit, and no bullet hole in the baby's head, my grandmother realized that the baby was buried alive. She did what she had to do. Afterward she came home and told us that she doesn't want to live any longer. She refused food, closed herself in her room and a few weeks later (at the end of our Passover holiday), my grandmother died. The young people who came to pay their respects said they envied her. They wished that they were in her place. I also felt relieved that Grandmother died a natural death and was not shot. I loved her very much and named my first daughter after her.

I must document an incident that happened after the second execution. One day, Gestapo soldiers arrived in our town and before we realized what was happening, militia men came to our door and arrested my father. He was one among approximately 14 men arrested that day. The panic in town was horrendous. We knew if they killed the men, shortly thereafter they would take away their wives and their children. I was thinking only about one thing, where could I possibly hide? What Christian family would be brave enough to hide me? At a time like this, one thinks about oneself. That day we were in agony fearing the worst, and the day seemed excruciatingly long. Toward the evening, we heard the front door of our house creek open, and my father walked in, pale as a ghost. He conveyed the following story:

As an interpreter for the Germans in WWI, my father spoke German very well. Consequently, he knew the rank of the German officers that took him away. My father overheard the Nazi officer exchanging words with one of the town militia.

"We are done with our paperwork. When we leave town, you will take care of those communists."

My father understood right away what this meant. With nothing to lose having been condemned to die, he approached the officer.

With respect for the officer's proper rank and in perfect German he said, "I heard you refer to us as communists. I am not a communist. As an officer, you understand that communists are Godless people. I am a religious Jew. How can I be a communist?"

He told my father, "You will say anything to get out of here."

My father pulled out his *titzit* (fringed undergarment) and showed it to him. "This is my sign of religious devotion to G-d. Only religious Jews wear it."

The officer took another look at my father and said, "Hmm...They made a mistake in you. You can go home."

My father thanked him politely and said, "I would check the others and see how many of them are religious people."

That night my father didn't know that the Nazi officers released all the men. The Germans left town and we were afraid that our militia, in retaliation, would come back and re-arrest and torture the men. That night my father slept in our garden between the potato rows so no one could find him. Certain death had been averted because of my father's quick thinking, which was one example of other actions that saved us.

Several weeks later an order came that we must provide ten men for labor in a neighboring town. This gave us a chance to send away Michel Patashnik, who had been hiding in our house, without jeopardy. My father was also chosen to fulfill the quota of ten. Mother, who was the clearest thinker in the family, realized that if she were left without a husband she would probably be selected for the next execution. Father also had a mild heart condition and Mother was scared he might collapse under the stress of hard physical labor. She told my oldest brother, Meyer, who was 15 years old, that he should go in place of Father. Just before they left my mother handed him a pair of *tefillin* (phylacteries) and told him, "My son, don't forget to pray and G-d will help you."

They were taken to Miadel (also known as Myadel), a nearby town. A few months later, Michel Patashnik, who was with my brother at that time, took decisive escape action that saved my brother's life. That is why Meyer was separated from the rest of the family during most of the war years.

Meyer and Michel's group had been organized in Miadel and forced into hard physical labor. News arrived to Miadel from a sympathetic German (we believed he was hiding the fact he was half Jewish) that the *einsatzgroupen* (killing units) were arriving to Miadel and Kobylnik to liquidate the Jews. An escape plan was discussed. Michel had already witnessed how the *einsatzgroupen* operated and knew they must act quickly. He was stronger and wiser than most men and told all the Jews to run away at night fall. He orchestrated a small group to run to the forest, and asked others to join him. Meyer, along with other boys and men, wanted to run back to their own towns instead. But Michel strong-armed Meyer into going with him. That night, under the cover of darkness, many Miadel Jews ran away into the forest. Against Michel's advice a few of the Jews from my town did return home. They were immediately apprehended and jailed. Without doubt, this maneuver saved Meyer's life. Those that did not go with Michel were brutally murdered just a day later.

8

Yosef Tunkevich

During this most frantic time, our town miraculously had several righteous gentiles who would put their own lives at risk to help us. My father was secretly, yet directly, approached by a farmer by the name of Yosef Tunkevich. Tunkevich had a piece of land about a fifteen-minute walk from our house. Not far from his house he had a barn that was close to a large, wooded area. Tunkevich was a short scruffy man, with a thick white mustache and bushy eyebrows to match his straight white hair.

Although Tunkevich had one adult daughter before I was even born, we understood she married someone he didn't like. In so doing, she moved away, and they became estranged. They had not spoken or seen one another for so many years, that Tunkevich appeared to be a man without children. His wife, however, did stay on and was dedicated to him.

Knowing that the Nazis had taken our cow, on occasion Tunkevich would leave a jug of milk on the stoop in back of our house.

While extending this kindness one day, he ran into my father and said, "Just to fight these Nazi beasts, I'm going to do everything I can to help the Jews."

He continued, "If you feel like you are in imminent danger and want to run and hide, I will leave my barn door unlocked. You will find a hiding place there beneath the straw."

Tunkevich said, "If they catch me, it's only me and my wife. The two of us." Glancing toward the ground, he said, "At least I am not jeopardizing the lives of children. I have no more children left!"

It was clear the loss of his daughter still ran deep, but this man took that sorrow, and turned it into something good, something lifesaving.

My father did not have a chance to take him up on that offer, but there was a rumor that a kind, good man was willing to help the Jews, and it spread among us. Later we learned that just before the final killing in our town, approximately ten people did manage to escape and hide in Tunkevich's barn. We heard he gave them rations of food and served as a look-out for a prolonged period of time. They survived because of him.

Another survivor, Asher Krukoff, who took refuge on Tunkevich's property (and translated for the publication of the *Memorial Book of Kobylnik*) recalls him this way:

> In the menacing sea of hatred and persecution there were a few individuals of genuine kindness, honesty and pure compassion. One such extraordinary individual in the dark sea of Jew hatred and persecution was the simple Ko-

bylnik Christian farmer, Yosef Tunkevich, who during the most difficult times under threat of death did not sell his soul to the devil and took a chance with his life to save Jews. Almost all surviving Jews of Kobylnik at one time or another found temporary sanctuary in his home and consequently survived the war. He received us initially and continued to help us when the whole town was occupied by the German military forces.

Several Kobylnik Jews were hidden by Tunkevich in his pigsty for 10 months in a dugout hole measuring three by three meters in size. On top of the dugout in the summer potatoes grew and, in winter, rye. The entrance to the dugout was in the pigsty through a hidden door, covered with garbage. From the door followed a tunnel about two meters long and through another small door made of thin metal, designed in case of a fire. In midday some light penetrated into the hole, but most of the time we sat in darkness. Only the good food provided by Tunkevich sustained our health.

In spring, Passover time, the dugout was full of water. We were forced to dig another hole and at night remove the water from both holes. We were steeped several weeks in wetness causing our deterioration while still staying alive. When Tunkevich would descend into the hideout he cried like a small child and failed to understand how we could survive in this environment.

Yosef Tunkevich was the only ray of hope in the great darkness that surrounded us. His name is mentioned by the survivors with holy reverence. He was the only symbol of human dignity and clear consciousness. We honor him by remembering his name.

Even with kind people like Tunkevich, most of us felt that there was no way to escape.

9

Foresight and Courage:
My Mother—A True Heroine

The Burgemeister's wife was an old friend of my mother. As I mentioned, when the Nazis took away our cow, we had no milk for my baby brother. The Mayor's wife would send her mother inconspicuously to bring him some milk. Recognizing this as a friendly gesture, Mother asked the Mayor's wife if she would like dresses made for her and her daughter, who was 18 years old at that time. When the *Gendarmes* came into our town, the Mayor's house became their meeting place and restaurant. My mother persuaded her friend that since she was now entertaining such important visitors, she and her daughter should look nice. She agreed, of course, and my mother started making dresses for them both. It was my mother's astute foresight that helped save our lives in the final moments before the implementation of the final execution.

After a while she even asked my mother to help her cook gefilte fish for her guests. The German *Gendarmes* loved my mother's fish. A German noticed my mother in the kitchen because she was wearing the Jewish star—he called her in and asked if my mother cooked the fish. She said, "Yes. I was asked to make it." He made her taste the fish first in front of him, and ultimately agreed— "very good fish."

For our town and a few other small townships, the final solution came on the holiday of Yom Kippur in 1942. When word reached the nearby town of Miadel that special *einsatz-groupen* had arrived to liquidate the Jews, the night of *erev* Yom Kippur 1942 no one went to bed. We children nodded off to sleep with our clothes on wherever we were. That same night, before the final solution, my mother dozed off for a little while and had a dream. She dreamt that she was preparing for a journey and was just about to leave the house, when her mother stopped her to hand over her husband's hat. She said to her, "Don't forget the hat." My Mother told us about the dream, but she could not interpret it at that time.

The tension and fear were palpable, and we had lost hope of any miracle. Where could a family with five small children run to hide? My 13-year-old brother, Hertzel, along with a couple of his friends decided to try. He said goodbye to my parents quickly and took off. Although there was nothing we could do, we were paralyzed by our emotions. Would Hertzel be alright running off with other children? Would we have a chance to escape? Was the end already here?

The Germans told us that we were being moved to be resettled in a larger town, but this was a lie to get us to leave our homes calmly and gather in the marketplace. The militia searched from house to house and with decisive manner ordered every Jew to assemble at the marketplace. When we were gathered, and not allowed to take anything with us, we realized this was the end. We were surrounded by the special "killing units" together with the *Gendarmes* from our neighboring town. As we walked to the marketplace, my mother noticed the Burgemeister's wife off to one side. My mother called out to her and said "Don't forget that I have in my house a couple of your unfinished dresses! Go and take them so that they will not get lost." I believe that one moment is what saved our family from execution that day.

Waiting in the marketplace we felt like trapped animals fearful and desperate for an escape. We were surrounded by Germans, along with the local, stone-faced, rifle-toting militia, and most of our Christian neighbors. I whispered into my mother's ear if it was alright for me to try and run. "Go my child, go!" I saw that all the Germans were speaking at one side of the gathering, and there was enough commotion among the group that I was able to slip away, cross the street, and enter the backyard of the next closest home. When I entered the house, I found an adult Jewish woman hiding there, behind the door. She quickly told me with some confidence that we were too close and that the Germans would be coming for us. She said, "Let's sneak through the gardens of these private properties and hide in the Jewish cemetery." We snuck out the back door of the house and got about two houses away when we were noticed by the local militia. Those militia men had heard a rumor that a Jewish neighbor hid money in his mattress, and with everyone else assembled in the marketplace, they were using this opportunity to check out that rumor and if it were true, take the money. But when they saw us, they immediately rushed toward us. I knew one of the two men and begged him to let me go, but he said, "Shut up Jewess!" At gunpoint he brought us back to the marketplace. Even though I did not succeed in getting away, the fact that I tried and got as far as I did, gave me extra courage to try and escape again.

My father overheard one of the German officers say to our militia chief, "Put them in the synagogue. It is the easiest way to finish them off."

My father alerted everyone to what was about to happen. My younger sister, Mina, became hysterical. She pleaded with my father to go and speak to the Nazi officer and beg him to shoot us instead. When my father walked closer to our Burgemeister he heard him discussing our fate with the Nazi officer in charge.

Burgemeister Wanzekowitz said, "The synagogue is too close to the other houses. Since most of the homes are wooden and it is a windy day, the whole village might go up in flames."

"All right then," said the German officer, "take them to the Dom-Ludovy"—the only public building we had in our town.

When they locked us up in that building the younger men quickly looked for a way to escape. The Baker, who was there without his family, opened one of the windows and jumped out. My father stood next in line to jump. The baker was apprehended instantly by one of our militia men. The German officer standing nearby told the militia man, "Take him away and get rid of him." When my father saw this, he backed off and came back to us and told us what happened. (I always wondered how my sensitive father might have felt if he had managed to escape through the window, without his wife and children, knowing we would have been shot that same day.) At a moment of indisputable doom, every person was desperate. Even I tried to escape from the marketplace. The Germans boarded up the windows.

I still have strong memories of the slaughterhouse. One of our militia men came in, grabbed a few men and took them away. Through the slats of the boarded up window we could see that they were given shovels to carry. We knew right away that they went to dig our grave. The old Rabbi and his wife were seated on a bench.

He called my father over and told him in resignation, "Swirski, it is time to say *vidui*," a prayer before one's death.

My soft-spoken father uncharacteristically reacted in anger. Looking at the Rabbi with wide, intense eyes, "Rabbi, who will say *vidui* for my infant son?" He turned and walked away.

To everyone else, this would have appeared to be disrespectful, and my father was never disrespectful to our Rabbi. But this literal life-ending crisis made my believing father question the Jewish customs and his own faith.

When the Jewish men returned and told us where they made them dig the ditch, we knew what our last route would be. At that time, at the end of September 1942, I was 11 ½ years old. I was very skinny and a good runner. I immediately started scheming what I would do when it would be my turn to be executed. Knowing the landscape well, I could envision the walk to that freshly dug grave. On the left side of that road, after the little bridge, there was a row of large trees. I planned to wait until we passed the bridge and then start running toward the trees. I knew that they would probably shoot me in the back, but I would rather die running than undress, walk up to the ditch, and be shot on top of everyone before me. As I was thinking and planning for myself, I suddenly caught sight of my mother, standing nearby with my baby brother in her arms. I realized then that she couldn't run with the baby even if she had wanted to.

I was startled from my daydreaming by an opening of the main door. They let in two more people: one of my mother's best friends (the Baker's wife) and her daughter, who was my best friend, Rachel. They came to join us willingly without being forced. She told my mother the following story:

She and her daughter, Rachel, were hiding in the bakery loft. When the Christian people from our village came in to rob their home and steal their belongings, she overheard them say, "They already killed the baker."

"It was then I realized I have no place to hide. I would rather die with everyone together."

My Mother was visibly angry with her friend. "You had no right to bring your daughter to the *akeida* (slaughter)."

I locked eyes with my friend. There were no tears, only fear. I sat down on the floor, closed my eyes, and thoughts came into my mind about my friendship with dear Rachel. We lived on the same street only one house away. On the way to school we always held hands. She always came to our house to do her homework with me, and I accompanied her to her house afterward, again holding hands. We were the same age.

Moments later a commotion began. Everyone started pushing toward the door. As I opened my eyes, I saw the German officer Kiel standing at the door with a short list in his hand. Kiel's face was familiar to us. He was part of the *Wermacht* from the German garrison in Miadel. He used to come to Kobylnik, issue all kinds of orders and was entertained by our Burgemeister, and his wife and daughter.

He started calling out names from the list. The person whose name he called would push himself to the door with his wife and children. "You can go home," he said.

He did so to several families whose husbands had trades such as tailor, mechanic, and cap-maker. We knew my father had no such trade, so we didn't get our hopes up that we might be one of the lucky ones let out. At the very end of the list, he called my mother's name. My mother, with the baby in her arms, grabbed my father and the rest of us and approached the door.

Kiel looked at my father and asked, "Who is this?"

"My husband," my mother said. "Well," Kiel said, sizing him up, "he looks strong enough. He can chop wood for me."

He turned to my mother and asked her, "Are you the seamstress in town?" She said, "Yes."

"I want dresses made for my wife. I will let you live a few weeks longer."

My brother's memory is better than mine; what happened next was relayed to me by him. We were four children with my parents. All the other families that were let out had only two children. Kiel said to my mother, "Only two children;" my mother was to choose which two of her four children to take with her. She said *"Alle vier"* (all four). And he let us all go out! I ran home as fast as I possibly could before he changed his mind and two of us would have to go back into the slaughterhouse. The trauma may have blocked it from my memory.

When we arrived home, the house was totally empty. All our belongings had been hauled out and put in the warehouse at the end of town. When darkness fell, my uncle Yesheya and his son Irwin appeared. He told us that his wife demanded he take his youngest son and hide in the barn loft. Yesheya's wife, my Aunt Frumell, along with their two daughters, Sheindal and Nechama Devorah, were among those who were awaiting execution in the Dom-Ludovy. We tried to contact them by bribing one of the militia men with money if he would free my aunt and her two daughters. After a while he came back and told us that the place was guarded by German soldiers, and he couldn't do it. (Frumell and Yesheya's third daughter, Malka, had been given to a distant cousin to raise because she was unable to have children, which was not a very uncommon occurrence. Unfortunately, Malka was also eventually killed.)

That night we hardly slept a wink. Father had to remove himself to another room to avoid showing his mood. We were all heartbroken. The kids lay down on the floor and dozed off into a shallow sleep. The adults whispered quietly and had to decide what to do with my uncle and his son. Again, my mother was the clear thinker. "They will come with us," she said without registering their presence. My mother realized that she would need her sewing machine in order to sew the dresses that the Nazi officer wanted. She decided that first thing next morning she would go to the militia station and ask for permission to reclaim her sewing machine. As dawn broke, we sat motionless. Our silence was broken by the first gunshots. Mother went outside all the way to the end of our garden. She saw in the distance moving figures. She came back into the house and told us that they started the executions. With every shot we heard I imagined whether this was my cousin or my girlfriend, Rachel, who was killed. We were numb with fear, understanding they could change their minds and come back to execute us. There was no place we could hide with a 15-month-old baby.

When the shooting ended, my mother went over to the police station, where she found Kiel, the Nazi officer, and asked for permission to reclaim her sewing machine. He handed her a note which gave her written permission and she went directly to the warehouse where they kept the belongings of all the Jews that were just killed.

As my mother approached the warehouse, she overheard two people arguing. A woman said, "Eva was my best friend! She would have wanted me to have her sewing machine."

The militia man told her, "I am in charge here and I am taking it for my mother."

As they argued about who would inherit my mother's sewing machine, my mother walked in with her permission slip to reclaim it. Without acknowledging any emotion, the woman turned around and asked my mother, "Eva, if they would have killed you this morning, would you want me to have your sewing machine, or Kolya?"

During the war years we never dared to talk back to a Christian person, realizing they could report us for any real or fictitious transgression to our militia. But my mother was so full of utter pain having just witnessed the killing of all the remaining Jews in town that she found the courage to answer back.

She said, "Helka, I heard you say we were best friends. You are right. We have lived on the same street all our lives, helped each other whenever we could. You knew when the Germans came, they took away my cow. You knew that I had a baby 10-days before the war started. Did you come by even once to offer me some milk for the baby? Is this how best friends behave?"

The woman was speechless. She didn't know what to say. They were both in shock. Mother did end up getting back her sewing machine and brought it home with the help of another person, as it was too big for her to carry by herself.

That same day, in the afternoon, we left our part of town for good. As we were leaving, we found on our doorstep a jug of milk and a loaf of bread. We understood that Helka left it. Kindness and caring do not come naturally to some people. It must be taught at any age.

10

Miadel Ghetto

After Yom Kippur in 1942 (with the exception of those few useful Jews and their families given a short reprieve), the last one hundred and twenty Jews from our village of Kobylnik were executed by the Nazis with the help of our local militia men. The militia continued to oversee us few remaining Jews in Kobylnik. The next day the Christian farmers were ordered to take us to the neighboring town of Miadel, each with their own horse and buggy. They loaded mother's sewing machine onto the wagon. As we started to move out of our town, we did not turn our heads to see what we were leaving behind, but we felt something approaching. In seconds we heard barking and looked back to see our dog Mooshka, eager and wide-mouthed racing to catch up to us. He was quick and spry and easily reached us, jumping swiftly into our wagon. We broke into tears witnessing the devotion of our pet. That spark of emotion enabled a tiny, yet welcome, release from the trauma of the execution. We all hugged and kissed

Mooshka—producing a moment of joy in our heavy-laden hearts. We knew that we could not keep him, so we asked the farmer who was taking us to Miadel if he would take care of him. He reassured us that he would. The short trip to Miadel was filled with great anxiety and fear of the unknown. The small ghetto of only useful Jews was created there right next to the *Gebitscomisariat* (German Headquarters).

The Miadel Ghetto consisted of two rows of homes facing each other. On one side of the street the houses remained empty, from those already murdered. We populated the other side. We were assigned to the last house in the ghetto with two windows that faced away from the garrison. Those windows had been boarded up with planks of wood restricting almost all natural light in the room. Only narrow beams of light pierced the room between the planks. Four Kobylnik families had been grouped together in this one house, we believed because each family had children. When all the daily work was done, most of the young children congregated in our house for that reason. The capmaker with his wife and two daughters lived in the kitchen area. Our family of six lived in the only bedroom. The painter with his wife and young daughter had a bed near the boarded-up windows, and my uncle Yesheya and Irwin slept in another corner. When we sat together, we convened in the living space.

It was an eerie feeling knowing that the inhabitants of this house were murdered just a couple of days ago and we were put in their place. The straw mattresses were still wet from the children's urine. Many of us were forced to sleep on the floor because there were not enough beds, and we gave the small beds with the straw mattresses to the men who had to go to work the next morning.

The Germans had full control over us with daily roll calls. Every day my father was taken away to work. I tried to be useful, so I joined the adult women who were knitting gloves for the German soldiers. I had learned to knit well.

My father came home from his work assignment one day and told us that he had met a Polish gentleman who was in charge of a warehouse where they were collecting plants for medicinal purposes. The plants were rotting, and he didn't know what to do for them. My father was a self-taught botanist and offered him help as long as he could obtain permission from the Germans for him to do so. Though she tried to prolong the dressmaking, once Mother was almost done with the dresses, we naturally became fearful. The next day, my father was assigned to work in that warehouse and helped revive those ailing plants which provided a great service. We felt a bit more secure knowing that father was "useful."

Because the Miadel Ghetto was now sheltering the few useful Jews that remained from Miadel and other nearby towns (like Kobylnik), there were people we knew from before the war. There was a widowed mother with four daughters we knew from Miadel. Her nephew had run to the forest early on and became a partisan freedom fighter. He had lived in a different town, but because he married a girl from Miadel he was close to their family. Rumors started to spread in the ghetto that one of the families was in contact with the Partisans and would probably try to escape. If an escape was being planned, the rest of us would be killed instantly. We realized it had to be the Miadel widow. Since I was the same age as one of her daughters, I was assigned to stay with them all day under the pretext that I came to play with her. They probably realized that we knew about their plans and talk of an escape dwindled. If someone knew the Partisans were planning an attack on the German garrison in Miadel, nobody shared it with us.

In a little over a week two trucks rolled into the ghetto with a list of people to be taken away. We were one of the families on that list. Of course, we were scared not knowing where they would take us, but we had no choice; when your name is called you must go. My father helped us kids onto the truck and was the very last person to climb in. With a great stroke of luck and quick thinking my father noticed in the distance the gentleman who had hired him.

He called out to him asking, "Don't you need my help anymore? They are taking us away! Go and ask the Gendarme that gave permission for me to work for you if we can have permission to stay."

The gentleman told the truck drivers to wait and ran to get permission for us to climb off the trucks. Another fortunate moment that saved our lives. To survive a little longer, one had to have the right skills, be proactive (like my parents were), and be very lucky. If my father would not have noticed his employer, we would have died like all the other people taken away on those two trucks. They were all from Kobylnik.

One morning at dawn we heard an awful lot of machine gun fire. It went on for about half an hour. My father ordered us to get dressed quickly and lie under the bed. When the shooting stopped my father walked up to the window to see what was happening. It was difficult to see out through the boarded-up window. Through the crevices he did notice a familiar face. My father knocked on the window and when that man heard him, he turned around surprised to realize that there were people left in the ghetto.

"What are you still doing here?" He quickly helped my father pry open the boards with his rifle, broke the window and told us to jump and run quickly through the marsh and into the forest.

"Our mission is accomplished; we are already retreating! We have guides in the forest, and they will tell you where to go."

Everyone jumped out with just the clothes on their backs. I was the very last one to jump because I looked for something to grab. In one hand I grabbed my big brother's old winter coat because I knew my mother had sewn gold pieces in the lining of that coat. When I approached the window to jump, I saw a thin blanket that was lying on the painter's bed that stood near the window. The painter, his wife and child were the first ones to jump out of the window. I was the last one and realized that my mother would need the blanket for my baby brother. At that same time, the Lithuanian and Polish militia ran into the church, up the steeple, and began shooting at us as we ran through the marshes. Running with my head tucked low and breathing heavily, the bullets were whizzing all around me. That winter coat was clumsy and heavy and kept me from running fast. Because I started to lag behind, I dropped the coat but held on tightly to the blanket. We finally reached the forest where one of the partisans took us to their hideout.

We were euphoric. For the first time in the last 16 months our lives were not in imminent mortal danger. We were hopeful. Maybe one of us would survive to tell the world what the beastly Nazis and their local collaborators did to our people.

That evening, the partisans slaughtered a cow. They cooked and fed us a big stew, something we had not eaten in a very long time. It is amazing how one good meal can improve your mood. We watched them work with a makeshift stove over a bonfire, cooking a big soup with the red meat, and divided it up among us. Because our bodies were not used to this type of nourishment, the nutrients were instantly sustaining to our systems. Afterward the commanding partisan leader approached and addressed us in a gruff and blunt manner.

"You gave your gold away to the Germans and now you want us to protect you? I need young men with rifles to help us fight."

Sneering, he continued, "You are middle-aged people with children. We have no use for you."

It was terrible news for our group. A heated and long discussion ensued among the Partisans that yielded a plan.

"The only thing we can do to help you is to give you a guide who will take you to a different distant forest. Because as soon as the Germans regroup tomorrow, they will bring out their dogs to sniff out your footsteps. They'll find you here, in this place, and we need to get moving in a few hours."

That guide took us far away, to another forest called Rusakowskaya Pushtcha, probably named after the nearest and largest village of Rusaki.

11

The Forest

Each family set up their own space with their own fire. The painter's wife noticed that my mother was carrying Sheldon in her shawl. She approached us and demanded that we give back the shawl. My mother explained to her how it was grabbed at the last moment of escape. I was enraged and told my parents not to give the shawl back.

"Tell her to go and get it where she left it," I said.

Even so, the painter's wife made a very big fuss about it, so my father had to step in. Being the honest man he was, he acknowledged that the shawl was hers and that both families had a great need for it. He felt the best way to resolve the matter was to cut it in half. It was a large shawl that women wrapped around their heads and upper bodies in the winter, so it was large enough to share. Half went to the painter's five-year-old daughter and the other half my mother used to wrap and carry baby Sheldon.

The painter's wife was not satisfied with this outcome and refused to speak with anyone from our family for many years. Both our families miraculously survived the war. Years later we met her on a trip to California. Her daughter was now in college. I didn't mention the shawl incident. I am still in touch with that beautiful woman who was once that little girl, who shared a shawl with my baby brother in those cold nights hiding in the forest.

November 1, 1942 was when we escaped from the ghetto and slept one night in a barn; we called it the *Kurhan*. It must have been one of the partisan's resting places. Now it was the second of November. We started out at dusk and walked all night with only short stops for a brief rest. My mother carried the baby in her arms, and Mina and I held on to her skirt. Meanwhile, the Germans were determined to find us. They sent planes that shot flares into the sky to light up the whole area. When we heard the planes near us, we quickly dropped to the ground and lay still until they passed. It was an excruciating night. Tired from the pace of walking and not sleeping, I felt like I could barely go on. With the stopping and starting Joshua held on to my father. Irwin (Itzke) and his father, Yesheya, were with us, but I don't remember seeing them until we arrived in the Pushtcha Forest.

A new saga of our survival began in the forest called Pushtcha. Pushtcha was a dense, uninhabited forest that covered an area approximately two miles wide and twelve miles long. Here too the partisans killed a cow and gave each of the families a chunk of meat. They helped us make a bonfire and told us to "guard it with your lives. If the fire will go out, you will freeze to death." We realized quickly how true this was. In this forest we found some individuals who escaped from other ghettos. Everyone tried to find a place near the fire. One specific person is still ingrained in my memory. He was a young boy about my age who escaped from an execution after his whole family was killed. He was in such shock that he hardly talked. My mother made some room for him near the fire and shared a few bites of food that we had. One night, when he was probably sick and tired of fighting for a place near the fire, he moved away about 10 to 20 yards and fell asleep under a tree. In the morning, we found him frozen to death. My father, along with another man, went to dig his grave. I overheard my father say, "What a lucky child. He fell asleep and didn't feel anything. He doesn't have to suffer anymore." I could not forget this. I kept thinking to myself, maybe when my parents will not watch, I should do the same thing and that would bring an end to my misery. The boy's grave had to be shallow because even though the first snow had not yet fallen, the ground was already completely frozen. The first snow came one week later.

It was almost impossible to fall asleep. We would lie around the fire wearing the light clothes we had escaped in, and some people used a small log to support their heads. The front of our bodies would be burning and the back freezing. No matter how many times we tried to turn, we could not stop shaking from the cold. I was eleven and a half years old at that time, understanding very little about life.

I remember asking my father in earnest, "If I continue shaking like this, will my soul jump out of my body?"

Maybe now you might understand why I wished to fall asleep and not wake up again like that little boy. A quiet death was preferred to this misery.

Shortly thereafter my father made a lean-to styled shelter in the hope of creating a little bit of relief from the snow. There was no shortage of wood. Many of the smaller trees had fallen and Father collected sturdy trunks and other large branches to create the framework of a wall that was later covered with evergreen branches. It had three sides and was only big enough for us four children to squeeze in tightly. My younger twin siblings, Mina and Joshua were sandwiched in the middle, flanked by my cousin, Irwin and me. We lay down on the ground inside the lean-to hugging each other for warmth. The two in the middle fell asleep, but Irwin and I, on the outside, were freezing. I tried to roll over to get some body heat on my back, but then my front froze. I was miserable, and even woke my younger siblings hoping to exchange places, but they would not move. Ultimately, I had no choice and returned to the bonfire.

The food situation was just as bad as the cold. We found out where the nearest villages were located and at night we would go begging for food. My father and brother, Joshua, were the main food suppliers. One always took along a child, to emphasize how desperate our situation was to the farmers. We baked the few potatoes they would bring back in the bonfire and divided them up equally for everyone in the family.

If the cold and the hunger were not enough misery, we became infested with lice. When not working to collect snow or wood, or beg for food, we often passed the time picking the lice out of each other's hair daily. It was impossible to fall asleep from the itching. My mother would take off our clothes one piece at a time and shake it over the fire. We could hear crackling as the lice fell into the fire. This kind of delousing gave us a very short respite from the constant itching. A man named Tilis, who escaped from a nearby town, was a barber who brought with him a manual hair clipper. My mother asked him to cut off our hair so that she could free our heads of lice. It worked for a while but left us with bare heads in the bitter cold and we didn't even have a rag to cover our heads. On windy days the air slashed our skin leaving it raw. When I think back on this time, I have no idea how we survived the cold.

One night I fell asleep too close to the fire. While turning in my sleep I inadvertently moved my foot into the flame, and it burned my shoe. The shoe leather scorched and became hard as a rock. It cut into my flesh and my foot started to bleed. We had no choice but to cut the shoe off and I was left in the cold winter barefoot. Luckily, a man from a nearby bonfire gave me a potato sack. We cut it in half and tied the rags around my feet. On our next begging trip to the village my mother took me with her. When we knocked at the first door, a woman opened the door and immediately saw my misery. She invited us into her house, took off my wet rags, finding icicles on my feet; I didn't feel pain until the woman started warming them up. Then it felt like someone was sticking needles into my flesh. The woman gave me dry rags and a pair of *laptze* booties for my feet. Those booties were knit from string. Tears rolled down her face from the moment she started tending to me. Her tears were those of sympathy for my situation, but also because the booties she gave me belonged to her son who had died. I never forgot the kindness of that woman.

12

The First Winter and Blockade

There is no doubt that the first winter was the hardest. Food was so scarce that in the beginning we sometimes had only a few small potatoes a day. The division of food was always equal among our family. I realized quickly that if I ate all my potatoes early in the day, by nighttime I was so hungry that I couldn't fall asleep. I decided to hide one potato for the evening, but when evening came and I went to retrieve it, it was gone. I had to assume that either my brother or cousin found it and ate it. My new plan was to hide one potato in my clothes. In the evening when I took it out to eat my sister would stand directly in front of me and with a look of despair she would cry, "I am hungry." I could not bear her moaning and felt I had no choice but to give her a piece of my potato. Many decades later when we were living in New Jersey and had all the food we needed, my sister would visit me frequently and often brought a gift.

"Why are you bringing me gifts for no reason?" I asked, and she would jokingly reply, "It is payback for the pieces of potato you gave me the first winter in the forest."

Night after night we saw fewer bonfires as they slowly extinguished. The younger people moved away and made "dugouts," underground bunkers for shelter. Before long ours was the only bonfire left. It felt like this was going to be the end of our lives. Nobody wanted to be near a family with a little baby. Only one elderly couple from a different town who escaped remained with us. They were probably in their sixties but, back then, to us they looked elderly. That old man confessed to my father that he had some gold coins which he brought with them and proposed to my father, in exchange for sheltering the couple, he could use the money to find someone to help make us an underground dugout. They were too old to go begging in the villages.

I don't remember exactly how it happened, but with my father's initiative and help from some other younger people on the run, we had a new underground shelter made possible by the gold coins of the elderly couple. That money was also used to buy a small metal potbelly stove that measured approximately two feet high and 18 inches wide, with a little door to put wood inside. Its exhaust pipe fed through the roof of our dugout, and it kept us warm. Our *pushtcha* was thick with very tall trees so any smoke we created dissipated before it could be seen. We shared with the old couple every bit of food that we brought from the village, but they didn't last too long. First the wife died, and the husband shortly thereafter.

In 1942 the Eastern European winter was officially documented as the coldest European winter of the century, with temperatures well below the already frigid conditions expected. Before we knew it, we were knee-high in snow with only the clothes we wore at the time of escape. Much later we learned that these same severe winter temperatures caused German tank engines to lock up, and in some cases were inoperable.

A few more bunkers sprang up in the area. I could see them about 100 yards from our shelter, so I was able to walk over. As a child, it gave me some comfort because I had someone to talk to and share my fears.

Apparently, someone in the nearby village told the Germans where we were hiding. They were so hell-bent on capturing every Jew that they brought in extra reinforcements and created a chain of foot soldiers that surrounded our *pushtcha* and advanced step by step searching for us. We decided that anyone who saw a German or heard a gunshot should start screaming—a signal for the rest of us to run and hide. These human lines in the forest swept through trying to uncover every soul.

When we heard gunfire, mother grabbed the baby and we all started running after her, deeper into the forest. We were like lost and frightened animals reacting to every sound and movement, our senses on overdrive. When we heard shots in the distance, we ran in what we thought was the opposite direction. When the shooting came toward our direction, we did everything we could to get away. We were running in knee-high snow in what appeared later to be circles all morning long. I remember feeling as though I could not move another step.

My father, who had a heart condition, suddenly stopped and told my mother, "You and the children try to escape. I can't move anymore."

That stop probably saved our lives. If we had gone any farther, we would have run into the German chain of soldiers that surrounded the whole forest.

Moments later my father noticed a man lying in the snow a short distance away. He had a gun in his hand. It was a Russian partisan who was wounded in a previous battle and his comrades could not carry him. The Germans were already so close that we could see their green uniforms in the distance. My father pleaded with the partisan to shoot him. Father knew that as a male, if he would be taken alive, they would torture him to death. The partisan numbly apologized, "I have only one bullet and I need it for myself." He told us to get away from him, because if we stayed with him, we were doomed. With our last bit of strength, we moved far away in the direction of a young outcropping of evergreens. When we got there, we crawled under the lowest branches covering the ground.

Once we were hidden, we heard the injured partisan begin singing a Russian patriotic song. When the Germans were in his direct sight, we then heard a shot ring out. The partisan took his own life. Hearing that shot echo from nearby, the Germans broke ranks and ran toward the sound to investigate. This left us outside the German deadly chain hiding under the evergreens.

When evening came and the Germans retreated from the forest, we found our way back to our bunker. As we trudged back in the snow, we had a moment to reflect. It was an excruciating day, without a drop of food to eat. Only then did we realize that our baby brother Sheldon, who was now 18 months old, had not cried once. He instinctively understood our imminent danger. When we finally found our bunker, it was clear the Germans had been there. They poured gasoline on our few potatoes left behind and exploded a hand grenade inside the shelter to destroy it. I don't remember where we slept that night.

The next morning, people came out of their hiding places and started to compare stories. Others were shocked to find that my family was all still alive. My father found a family from Miadel. They agreed to let us stay with them until we repaired our bunker. It was so small and packed inside it was hard to breathe. I actually remember fainting from lack of air, and they carried me out to revive me on the snow. With the help of others, in a few days father repaired the damage to our dugout, fixing the exhaust pipe and stove and reinforcing the sides. With our bunker now fixed, we returned to our place.

One can get used to almost anything. Our dismal existence in the hole in the ground felt almost normal compared to the unprotected and miserable winter in the *pushtcha* earlier that season. Had we not been living under the constant fear of capture by Nazi soldiers, and those that helped them, that hole under the ground might have felt like a home.

The partisans sought and found which farmer informed the Germans of our hiding place and they burned down his house. He escaped to the city of Vileika. In this cold climate it was customary that farmers bury their potato crop in large pits covered with straw and then soil to prevent freezing. They would uncover one pit at a time, as needed, for their winter use, and as seed for the next season. Someone showed us where that informant's potato pits were and all of us made several trips that night to grab as many potatoes as we could carry. I remember making two trips myself that night. I could barely stand on my feet. Mina stayed behind to take care of baby Sheldon. Before the first blockade, we had only a few small potatoes a day for each person, but now we felt like we had a potato feast awaiting. The horrible conditions of that winter cannot be overstated.

* * *

After the first blockade, we were constantly on guard. Every sound we heard was cause for investigating to see whether strangers or Germans were sneaking up on us. We were four young children: my cousin Irving, my brother Joshua, my sister Mina, and myself. We didn't count the baby because he was always with Mother.

We already had a dugout with a platform that served as a foundational floor made from young birch trees. We had to find a way to keep ourselves busy. The first order of the day was to get out into the sunlight and delouse ourselves. The infestation of lice was the worst menace to us; so as not to lose our sanity, we made a game of it. We would take off one article of clothing at a time and count, who could find and kill the most lice. We even started to joke; "The lice will probably eat us alive before the Germans will kill us." The next thing to occupy our time was searching for pieces of wood to feed the fire. This was a tough job in the winter when everything was covered with snow. We found a clearing in the forest where the farmers prepared wood for the winter. The wood was seasoned and burned easily. We felt guilty about taking their wood, but it was a lifesaving necessity.

Getting water for boiling the potatoes or cooking a soup if we had something to add to the potatoes was a big undertaking. The snow that we would collect was mixed with all kinds of impurities and it would melt down to very small amounts. We found a hole in the ground that the farmers dug up for watering their horses. The water in that hole was cleaner than the melted snow. It was about half a mile from our dugout, which made for a challenging errand. The old tin can we carried the water in had no handle and our fingers would freeze stiff. Taking turns carrying the can, usually two kids went to retrieve the water at a time.

After some time, a few other dugouts appeared near us. One of them had kids our age. On a quiet evening, we would go over there to socialize and sing songs of hope that we learned from the partisans. It raised our spirits a little and was intended to help us forget our miserable existence for even a short while.

One very cold winter evening, when my sister was moaning that she was hungry, I got tired of listening to her and walked over to a nearby dugout. I found the same situation there only the moaning came from the older sister. The younger sister was my age and was also called Chana. The two of us conspired to do something about it. We would go to the nearest village, which was about three kilometers away, and see if we could get some food for our sisters. I can't remember if we told our mothers about our plan. In any case we headed out into the freezing night holding hands, the wind penetrating through our thin tattered clothes, and the night sky settling into a dark cobalt blue. We were shaking continuously from the cold bitter air. Suddenly in the distance we noticed four tiny lights. At first, we had no idea what it was, and as we looked closer, we realized they were the eyes of two wolves. My friend's reaction was, "Let's run!" I held her hand firmly by my side and would not let her run. With nervous whispered breath, I told her that my father taught me that you cannot outrun a wolf and it will not attack a human being unless he is very hungry. We walked as quickly as we could but didn't dare run. We made it to the edge of the forest with the wolves following us. We could still see their glowing eyes against the gloomy backdrop of the forest. Once we were out in the open field closer to the village we ran as fast as we could. The wolves did not leave the forest. Our hearts raced; we were scared to death.

Because the winters were so fierce, most homes had a covered animal pen attached to the back of the house. There the smaller animals sheltered from the cold. We walked up to first house we came upon, passing by the pigs and chickens. We knocked lightly on the back door of the house. The family was having dinner by a very dim light.

The farmer looked at us and said, "Are you crazy in this kind of weather? We wouldn't even let our dogs out today. Besides, I heard the Germans are at the other end of the village."

We later understood he was trying to scare us because we were too young at that time to realize that in this kind of brutal cold Germans would not come out to a remote village. He gave us each a few potatoes and we left. On the way out, walking through the animal pen I smelled warm potatoes. The farmer had boiled the tiny potatoes and fed them to the pigs. I stretched out my hand and grabbed a handful of the warm potatoes and ate them on the spot. The pigs began squealing and we ran off as fast as we could. We didn't continue going through the village but turned back to the forest. On the way back we did not encounter the wolves. When we finally came back to our dugouts, we got a terrific scolding from our mothers. They thought we were lost in the forest at night. We never tried such an adventure again.

Most of the food supply was foraged by my father and my brother Joshua. They usually went to the villages and tried to obtain whatever they could just to keep us alive. We survived each day as it came, and honestly it was hard to measure time. Days turned into weeks and weeks unfolded into a month.

Yisrael Leib left our forest after this first blockade. My father asked to speak with him and told him where he had hidden the 500 rubles that mother's cousin gave him, along with our jewelry—just in case we didn't survive.

13

The Second Blockade

The second blockade occurred after the snow started to melt, so I am guessing it was in the early spring. During this time, we heard a few gunshots ring out and started to run away in the opposite direction. Mother grabbed the baby, and I grabbed a small bag of crusty bread, which we had set aside for emergencies. We ran directly into the swamp that was about a half mile away from our dugout. Dredging through the knee-deep water we jumped from one outcropping of raised earth to another until we finally found a tree stump that was surrounded with dry land. Mother motioned to me to soak one of the pieces of dry bread in the swamp to soften for the baby. We gave it to Sheldon to suck, and in so doing we kept him from crying and giving away our location. We slowed our breathing, and, in the distance, we could hear the Germans talking, but they did not want to enter the swamp. We waited in stillness and silence for their retreat. Toward that evening, when the shooting stopped, we returned to our dugout. Once again, the Germans had poured gasoline on the potatoes that we left behind and damaged our dugout. We were getting used to being without food for a day or two. We were just glad to be alive.

The shelter was not completely destroyed, so at first father thought we could sleep there. But it soon became clear that the baby needed more warmth, so he left our marred dugout seeking a place for Mother and the baby. There was a near-by bunker with a burning fireplace that was not discovered during the blockade, but a mean woman there did not want to permit my mother entry, even though she had the baby. "If we let Chava and the baby in, the other children will find excuses to come in as well." Others there insisted on letting Mother in, and she squeezed into a small space by their fire with Sheldon on her lap. That woman was right about us. We were freezing and tried every way we knew how to get close to Mother to take advantage of even a little warmth.

In that early spring blockade, Aaron from Svir (a village 12 kilometers southwest of Kobylnik), with two of his sons and a nephew had gone to beg for food and decided to sleep over in a kind farmer's bathhouse. Early the next morning Germans arrived at that village looking for partisans. The soldiers pushed into the farmer's home with such authority and aggression that fearing for his own life, the farmer told them that Jews were in his bathhouse. Aaron and his boys were caught in that place and all four of them were shot by the Germans. The farmer was ordered to bury the Jews, but when he went to collect the bodies, he found only three bodies. The father, Aaron, was not there. Having been shot and left to die, when the coast was clear and Aaron was still conscious, he crawled into the farmer's barn and hid there until the evening. The next day he regained consciousness and managed to crawl back to the forest. He was absolutely unrecognizable. The Germans had shot him in the back of his head and the bullet came out through his cheek. His whole head was so swollen that we were sure he would die. Hearing about this, my mother ran directly to their dugout to see if she could help. No one knew what to do. My mother took off her cotton undershirt and tore it into strips and started boiling the rags. She lightly bandaged his head with the new clean bandages to stop the bleeding. Everyone contributed whatever they could to aid his recovery. Pieces of bone started coming out from his cheek and the puss was squeezed out daily. It finally started to heal. Aaron survived the war, and after the creation of the state of Israel he and his wife and their only remaining youngest son moved there. Aaron's son was killed serving in the Israeli army during the Sinai campaign. Aaron and his wife died of old age with broken hearts.

With the melting of the snow, a new scourge surfaced—typhoid fever. Lice were the biggest carriers of this disease. My younger brother Joshua, then 10 years old, came down with it first. It was still easy to find snow even though it had started to melt. My sister and I collected some to put on his burning forehead. Mother boiled every drop of water she gave him to drink. As his temperature finally broke, the third blockade erupted.

14

The Third Blockade

As always Mother grabbed the baby and started to run. Father took my brother Joshua, who could not yet walk still weak and recovering from typhoid fever and carried him on his back. My sister, Mina, and I followed our parents. Suddenly planes appeared low overhead and started to shoot at every moving object. We heard bullets whizzing through the air. Holding the baby my mother stood motionless pressing her body behind a large tree. The rest of us followed her example. We spread out behind trees and stood as still as possible.

My baby brother was almost two years old by then and had started to talk. My mother held his head close to hers; she later explained to us so that if a bullet hit them, they would die together. The planes continuously swept the forest and shot at everything moving. Mother told us that the baby whispered into her ear, "Mommy, don't throw me away. I will be quiet." We didn't realize how Sheldon listened and observed, fully comprehending our situation. Early on, when hiding in the first blockade the son of another woman hiding not far from us was less fortunate. She found her son too heavy to carry anymore and a hindrance to hiding. She abandoned the child. That abandoned child was later found alive by the partisans and returned to its family. That mother suffered enormous stigma and shame from the memory of leaving her child behind. Miraculously, all the members of my family lived through the third blockade, though there were substantial casualties in another part of our forest.

My cousin, Irwin, was not with us during the third blockade. His older brother, Yisroel Leib, had left our *pushtcha* after the first blockade, and came back to retrieve him earlier. It turned out that Yisroel Leib did find his father Yesheya's hiding place in a small forest not far from Kobylnik. He would not tell us where it was because nobody wanted us nearby, fearing trouble with the baby, not even my uncle, Yesheya, and first cousin, Yisroel Leib.

There were so many people killed in the third blockade that word of no survivors reached Yisroel Leib. Assuming that we were killed, and now knowing that there was money hidden at our old home, he found his way to Tunkevich and tried to make a deal with him. He said, "I know the money is buried somewhere under our house. If you can find it, we can share it." Promising nothing Tunkevich was able to go there and dig around. We later understood that he did find the 500 rubles and more but did not reveal this fact to Yisroel Leib. We believe Tunkevich kept it. Though it would have been useful, Tunkevich more than earned the right to this money, helping and saving many of our town's Jews.

After the third blockade, my father realized that we needed to find another hiding place. Since the Germans knew that Jews were hiding in this *pushtcha*, sooner or later they would find us. After six months we left our dugout and set out for an unknown destination. After about half a day of walking it started to rain. We had no shelter or place to hide. As the sky grew darker and the rain intensified it poured continuously for about 30 minutes. We were all soaked to the bone. Everything was wet. After the rain finally subsided, starting a fire to dry out our clothes seemed almost impossible. There were other Jews who fled the *pushtcha*, but nobody had a match to start a fire. My father picked up two rocks and a few pieces of bark from a birch tree. Birch bark is very thin, sometimes even thinner than paper, and usually catches fire easily. My father started rubbing the rocks against each other and another man stood by with the birch bark. It took a while because of the damp conditions, but as soon as sparks started to fly from the rocks, the bark from the trees caught fire. We had been shaking from the cold and I remember hearing all our teeth chatter uncontrollably. That bonfire felt so good, and we were able to slowly dry out our soaked clothes. We spent that night under the open sky, near that miraculous fire.

The very next day, my mother, my sister Mina, and I all came down with typhoid fever.

Once again, my father quickly managed to build a lean-to with evergreens as a roof and all three of us were somewhat sheltered from the wind and rain. My sister and I got better in a few days, but my mother's temperature would not break. Even though it was already spring, we could still find a little snow much deeper in the forest. We put the snow on her forehead and let her suck on a cleaner piece of hard-packed snow. We were all sure that she was going to die. While my mother was sick, our two-year old brother walked over to another bonfire and, in a matter-of-fact way, told the people there, "My mother is dying. Give me something to eat!" Those kind people returned Sheldon to us.

For a whole week Mother had a very high fever and she continued to sweat and hallucinate on the ground of that lean-to. Then, what appeared to be out of nowhere, she opened her eyes and told my father if she had a piece of butter she would get well. My father and brother immediately took off for the nearest village. Father told a farmer his predicament and the farmer gave him a piece of butter. We realized this was an extraordinary act of kindness. We had absolutely nothing to give him in return, and a piece of butter during the war years was not easy to come by and was highly valued.

Mother slowly swallowed the piece of butter and after a short while she asked for help to rise and walk out of the lean-to. The butter had caused her to move her bowels. She had not stood up on her feet for over a full week. Though very weak, she told the family that she would live. She told us later that she had a vision when she was hallucinating from the fever that a piece of butter would cure her.

The location where we had stopped to build the post rainstorm fire and where we became ill with typhoid fever was a temporary forest location on the way to find a more permanent hiding place. In this place we were surprised by a few Jewish visitors. A group of young men, mostly from our village, who escaped from the Vilna Ghetto, were looking for us. Among them was Yesheya's son, our first cousin Hertzke. He was the youngest in the group, either 18 or 19 years old at the time. They explained how they escaped from the Ghetto and that they were looking to join the partisans.

15

Hertzke

Like my oldest brother Meyer, Hertzke's path was different from ours. During the Kobylnik lockdown my cousin Hertzke had been sent off to work hard labor in the neighboring town. He was not one to sit around waiting for a miracle. He escaped and made his way to the Vilna Ghetto. That ghetto was an enormous place overrun with captured Jews. He sought out the elite young freedom fighters who wanted to join the Partisans in the forest. Hertzke was almost too young to be considered, but he wanted to avenge the death of his mother and sisters; when the Germans decided to make our village *judenrein* (Jew free), they were murdered on September 22, 1942, along with the other 120 Jews. For that reason, he begged them to include him. He had heard a rumor that his uncle, David Swirski, was now the commander of the partisans, and he promised that if they took him along, he would be able to get his uncle to help them.

Months earlier, in the first *pushtcha*, the partisans were scouring the countryside for weapons when word reached my father. Because of his earlier job during the Russian occupation, he told the partisans that he knew specifically those people that were issued rifles for hunting. He agreed to show them which homes had the weapons. It was snowing and the partisans had a large sled drawn by horses. They set off for town and as they neared, father pointed out the homes. He did not exit the sled and waited alone there as the partisans entered the house and demanded the rifle from the farmer. There was quite a protest that no such rifle was available but having inside information the partisans were not dissuaded. Ultimately, they pointed to Swirski outside waiting in the sled, and explained they had this information about the issued rifle. The rifle was handed over. However, that farmer drew the conclusion that David Swirski was the commander of that unit of partisans, as he didn't even move from the sled. The rumor swept from house to house, until the rumor finally reached us through Hertzke.

Hertzke's arrival to our temporary forest location was a miracle sent from heaven.

My mother, my sister and I were too weak to walk a long distance. We needed to get away and find a better hiding place, preferably the area where my uncle Yesheya and cousins were hiding. Hertzke, our family hero, put the baby on his back and helped us all move on to our next destination. The walking was very slow. We had not yet recovered from the fever and had very little energy to walk far. My legs felt like tree trunks, and we had to rest often.

On this particular journey (I don't remember how) we found Juzef Talaika, another rare righteous gentile who, risking danger, helped Jews in our area. We arrived at his homestead. He and his wife treated us like honored guests. The first thing Talaika did was heat up his bathhouse and make us all take a bath, the first we had in six full months. I remember that one by one we took off our clothes and shook each article of clothing over the hot stove. Once again, we could hear the crackling of the lice burning as they fell from our clothes onto the hot stones. It was an oddly satisfying sound. Because we had nothing to change into, after bathing and dropping the lice, we put the same rags back on. At the same moment we were taking the rare opportunity to wash up, Talaika's wife was preparing us a meal of boiled potatoes and sour milk. We had not been treated like this since long before the war started. Juzef told us he was sheltering another Jewish family in this private forest, and we should go to join them. That other family turned out to be the same one we helped in the Pushtcha. It was Aaron from Svir who was shot in the head through his cheek and my mother helped with her last undershirt to bandage him. He, his wife, and youngest son were very glad to see us. We stayed in Talaika's (private) forest for only a few days. Then he told us it was time to move on to a safer place. His oldest son, Valodya, was our guide to cross a thick swamp and bring us to our uncle's hiding place.

Image Gallery

Rivka and Chava Gordon, circa 1920

David Swirski, pre-World War II

Chava, her sister Slava (seated), and Cousin

Yosef Tunkevich

Kobylnik, WWI

Townspeople of Kobylnik pre-war

Ann and Mina, 1945

Town of Miadel on the lake (Miadel Ghetto)

A general celebration in
Kobylnik in the 1930s

Typical pre-war oven in Poland

David and Chava Swirski and children, 1937. Upper row from left to right: Chava, Meyer, and David; lower row from left to right, Chana (Ann), Mina, Joshua (Jim), and Hertzel.

Zionist pioneers chopping wood in Kobylnik

Jewish partisan fighters including leader, Abba Kovner of the Vilna Ghetto (back row, center)

Ann, age 15, at a DP camp

Ann and Meyer, 1947

Ann's family at the DP camp, Wasseralfingen

Surviovors of Kobylnik after the liberation next to the mass grave

Medical cards for Chava, David, and Chana (Ann)

Ann and her cousin Irwin, 1948

Ann and Irwin, 1953

Ann, Mina, and bystander voyaging on the *Anna Salen*, 1951

Chava and David, Toronto, 1955

Bobby (Chava), in Elizabeth, NJ

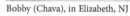

Ed Jaffe, 1949

Portrait of Ann at age 21 in 1952

Passover, 1954

Ed and Ann in Ontario, Canada, 1953

Ann, 1954

Nathan, Mina, Ann, and Ed in Toronto, 1953

Ann, Mina, and Sheldon, 1956

Ann

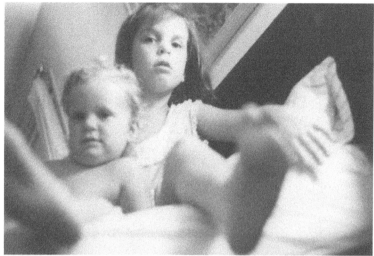

Linda and Rebecca, 1963

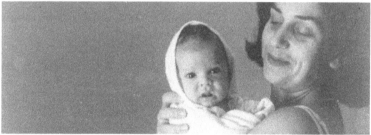

David and Ann, 1964

Linda, David, and Rebecca, 1966

Jaffe family, 1979

Ann's first return to Naroch (Kobylnik), 1994 with her brother Jim (Joshua)

Ann (4th from right) with her family, 2007

Front page news, 2010

16

The Partisan Zone

By the spring of 1943, the constant presence of Russian partisans was well known. They established a stronghold in a large rural area with dense forests. The Germans seldomly came to that area and when they did, it was only with a very large force to carry out a blockade. The partisans had established a system of communication with local villagers who would inform them if the Germans were near. Everyone referred to this place as "The Partisan Zone," and it was, by far, the safest location we had lived in during our time in the forest.

By the time we arrived at my uncle's hiding place in the Partisan Zone, my father was then in his mid-forties. There was enough room there, and we stayed in Yesheya's dugout. Father immediately constructed an elevated platform from seedling trees so that we would have a place to sleep other than on the bare ground. There were other dugouts nearby sheltering mostly Jews from our village. My father organized all the men to help and work together to dig a well so that we didn't have to drink water from the nearby pond. They also constructed a new and separate underground bunker that became our common bathhouse; we had to get rid of the lice that were a constant nuisance to everyone. We were filled with hope that there was a chance for some of us to survive. This place was in closer proximity to Kobylnik, which also helped in obtaining food.

Despite the recent bath at Talaika's place, we looked like people without shelter for over a year, worse than you can imagine. Our appearance had changed drastically. We could not comprehend how we appeared to others. We were clearly emaciated. We wore the same unlaundered clothes we started out with a year ago, that had been burnt and ripped by the elements. What was left of our clothes hung on our bones. We paid no attention to this. And the kindhearted barber living with us in the *pushtcha* with the manual clippers had long ago cut our hair back, because of the lice.

My father and brother, Joshua, went out for a food expedition to the largest nearby village. When a man answered the door of the first house, my father approached and asked, "Can you spare something?"

At first sight the farmer didn't know who stood before him (we were unrecognizable after so many months), but within seconds he recognized my father's voice and said, "Is that you Swirski?"

With slightly lifted brow my father said "Yes."

"What are you doing begging?" he asked.

My father replied, "I have no choice. I have nothing to give you in return. The Germans took away everything from us. My wife and the children are hiding in the forest without food."

Registering his shock and anger, the farmer shook his head from side to side telling my father, "Most of the people in this village know you. You are a respected and kind man. I will not let you lose your dignity begging."

He motioned quickly to his two sons and instructed them in front of Joshua and my father to "Go through the village and tell everyone that Swirski is here. Tell them they should contribute anything they can spare for his family."

My father's gratitude was hard to express but was acknowledged between the two honorable men. Remembering this event always brings tears to our eyes. The combination of our deprivation and helplessness, faced with this kind and generous act evokes strong emotion to this very day.

That afternoon my father and brother came back to our hiding place with bags full of food. I can't remember everything that was in those bags, but my mother immediately began to prepare and cook a black pea soup. On some previous begging trip to town mother noticed a broken pot in someone's garbage.

She asked if she could take it, and the person said, "It has holes in the bottom, and I have no use for it. Take it."

Mother found a way to stop up the holes with clay soil. We also had only one bent tin can and one broken spoon with which to eat the soup, so we took turns. When my turn came the black pea soup tasted like manna from heaven. I thought to myself, why didn't we cook black pea soup before the war? When the war will end, if I survive, all I want is enough black pea soup until my belly will be completely full. From that day on we were no longer starving, but we did continue to be hungry.

We even allowed ourselves moments of joy. We would run around the forest searching for animals, visiting other bunkers, and listening to the grown-ups telling stories from the past, and strategizing on what to do if the Germans would make another blockade. We decided that we would need an additional hiding place far away from the underground bunker in which we now lived.

My cousin, Hertzke, who joined the partisans, came to visit us occasionally on his return from a mission and would bring us something useful. One time he actually brought us a cow! In amazement we asked, "How did you get it?" Just as the war was breaking out, his father Yesheya had given one of his horses (that was stored in our barn along with the cow we had to give away) to a friendly Christian neighbor to hold for safe keeping. When Hertzke ran into him and saw their horse, the farmer assumed Hertzke wanted the horse back. Before Hertzke even said anything that poor farmer pleaded with him that the horse was all he had and could not give it up.

He bartered, "How about I give you a cow?"

That cow was slaughtered by Aaron from Svir; as luck would have it, he had worked as a butcher before the war. My brother remembers that one well-placed puncture to the top of the cow's head caused the animal to become paralyzed and fall to the ground. They quickly tied its legs together and swiftly slit the jugular in a manner that killed the cow with the least amount of suffering. It was remarkable to see the animal flung over a thick tree branch, as they skinned and carved it up. Mother cooked the meat every day and shared it with anyone else who was hiding in the woods with us. She even made salami from some of the meat, which would keep much longer and be able to feed us when other food was not available. She instructed me and my sister to take the intestines of the cow to the closest pond and scrub and wash it out as best as we could, leaving just the outer membrane. Others had collected fragrant vegetables from generous farmers.

Mother combined meat, fat, garlic, onions and somehow, she had some salt. She stuffed it into the intestines, cured and smoked it over the fire. Mother was amazing.

Also, during his visits, Hertzke regaled us with stories of his heroism. He had successfully derailed a train that was bringing supplies and German soldiers to the front lines of the army. One group was sent to plant dynamite underneath the train tracks. Someone needed to light the wick when the train was in sight. They chose Hertzke because he was young, agile, and Jewish. My cousin was fearless and was legendary among us. My second cousin, Hertzke's daughter, Hassida, lives in Israel, and has recorded everything she learned about his heroism from stories she heard firsthand from him and other family members who were with him in the forest.

At this time, we also met two very important Yiddish poets. They escaped from the Vilna Ghetto and came to the Naroch forest. They became part of a Russian contingent (Atrad) and were recording the history of the partisan accomplishments. They also continued writing Yiddish poetry. Not far from us, in one of the bunkers, were two sisters from the town of Svir who had been teachers before the war; the poets, Shmerke Katzerginski and Avrohom Shutzkever, considered them intellectual equals. They would visit their bunker and read their poetry to the educated sisters. Children my age were eager to see new faces from outside our forest, so we ran over there to sit down on the ground and listen to their poetry. Some poems we memorized by heart, and they became nourishment for our souls. Hope grew greater that some of us would make it out. After the war, these two poets became famous among Lithuanian survivors.

That same winter, a young couple from the village of Svir escaped from the Vilna ghetto. They arrived in our forest and moved in with the other people from Svir. They told us they had to escape because the woman was pregnant. The

Germans sent pregnant women to Panary (an execution site near Vilna). That pregnant woman became another attraction to occupy our time.

My father knew the young pregnant couple from Svir and would sometimes talk politics with them and discuss our chances of survival. Svir was only 12 kilometers from our village, and we had many relatives there. When the pregnant woman went into labor someone came looking for my mother to help with the delivery. Mother was an experienced midwife. By the time my mother got there she found someone else had arrived before her to help deliver the child. A healthy beautiful baby boy was born in the forest of Naroch.

We took care of our own health the best way we knew. For example, my father stepped on a nail one day and his foot became infected. The incident with Aaron from Svir taught my mother a great deal. First, she would squeeze out the pus from the wound. She sterilized cloth rags in boiling water to disinfect them. Then she wrapped the injured area with the clean bandages until the wound was healed.

A while later my mother began to feel unwell. She had developed a terrible toothache and tried to ignore it as long as she could. Eventually the infection caused her whole face to swell, until the excruciating pain was too much to bear. Having little choice, she decided to go to the nearby village to see if someone could help her. She took my brother Joshua with her for assistance and support. This story comes from my brother who witnessed the event firsthand. Some kind people were willing to point them in the direction of someone who could help her, a man named Martin. Martin had been an assistant to a medic during World War I, which made him the most capable of available people at the time. They found Martin working in a countryside workshop. When Martin took one look at Mother he said, "We have to pull the tooth." Mother agreed gladly. Martin set her in a chair and asked her to sit on her hands and asked my brother to get behind her and hold her head steady. He put a solid wood block in mother's mouth to keep it wide open. After he identified the ailing tooth, he pulled out a pair of his cleanest pliers that were stored in the leg of his right boot. He took hold of the tooth and with one swift movement pulled it out as quickly as possible. Blood instantly squirted out of Mother's mouth onto her clothes.

"Spit out the blood," he directed her and gave her some water for rinsing her mouth out, but the blood continued to flow at quite a pace. Martin told my brother to take care of her for a moment while he stepped outside to bring some leaves from a tree that was growing nearby. He had learned that those specific leaves had healing properties.

He handed her a bundle of the leaves rolled into a cylinder and told her, "Put some of this in your mouth along the wound and squeeze down hard. It will help."

The swelling started to shrink quickly. By the time Mother and Joshua returned to the forest she already was able to smile and did so most appreciatively. The pain was almost gone. We were forever grateful to Martin for easing Mother's pain and saving her from what might have developed into a critical situation. Only a few months later we were liberated by the Russian army on July 4, 1944.

In the late spring of 1944 rumors had reached us in the forest that the Germans were suffering one defeat after another on the Russian front. The thought of the Russians pushing Germans back, out of our territory, was happy news, though survival was still very much in question. We also learned that out of their hatred or desperation, retreating Germans were even more actively penetrating the forest looking for partisan fighters and hidden Jews. This news made the adults among us realize we needed a well camouflaged bunker where we might hide. The able-bodied men found a place not far from our current dugout so that we would be able to run and reach it when and if the critical moment came. It was a deep hole in the ground covered by a small gathering of shrubs. To get into it one had to remove the top, jump in, and then replace the shrubs over the top of the hole. Once it was set up, they tested the camouflage by walking the children through the area to see if we could find the hole. We eagerly ran around looking for it but could not find it. This satisfied the adults; the camouflage passed inspection.

As the news of the war front moved closer to our area, our parents showed the children where the hidden hole was located. We realized by the movement of airplanes and cannon fire that the front line was now very nearby. Every day and night we listened with dread as the sounds of the war front moved closer and closer. The uncertainty of pending discovery made us sick with anxiety and raw nerves.

One morning a farmer came running toward us and yelled, "The Russians are here! You are free!"

At first, we thought he was playing a cruel joke on us, but when he told us that he saw Russian tanks on the main highway, our tension was cut with quiet tears of joy. My 11-year-old brother Joshua and my 13-year-old cousin Irwin quickly ran off in the direction of highway.

When they returned to us in the forest they came bolting and screaming, "Yes, yes. They are Russian tanks!"

At that moment, our emotions were hard to put into words. Of course, we were overjoyed that we were able to live through the war to be liberated. On the other hand, we were keenly aware of just how few of us survived. Once the initial relief moved through us, our thoughts drifted sadly to all the people in our village who were murdered. If it was a victory, it was bittersweet at best.

17

Liberation

Rumors reached us that some German soldiers who could not keep up with the retreat were left behind and trying to hide in our same forest. My father alerted our whole family to be on the lookout.

He told us, "If you see a green uniform, immediately run to the hiding place."

Suddenly, someone started screaming, "Germans!"

My younger sister, Mina, grabbed Sheldon and ran quickly to the new hiding place. She pushed away the camouflaged shrub that served as its top and jumped into the hole with the baby. She did the best she could to cover it back up.

As the two foreign men continued to approach our area, we scrambled to escape screaming, "Germans!"

As they neared us, we quickly saw that these two men were laughing at us and said, "Don't you recognize us?"

They were two Jewish partisans we knew from our area who had just killed two German soldiers they found hiding in the forest. They took off their German uniforms and put them on themselves. It was a stupid way to play a trick on us. But once the momentary shock wore off, we were happy to see them. We sat to talk with them, and we discussed that it was probably time to leave the forest. There were too many Germans roaming the woods. We ended up spending the rest of the afternoon with them and were so distracted that we didn't realize that Mina and the baby were missing. When it finally dawned on us, our hearts sank, and our stomachs hurt. We all spread out to look for them throughout the whole area, but we couldn't find them. We became frantic. At that moment it occurred to my father that they might be hiding in the camouflaged hole in the ground. That is where we found them. When Father moved the shrub door from the hole, Mina was crying and shaking, hysterical with fear. It had been relatively easy to jump into the hole, but once she closed the top off, she wasn't able to open it. I believe this scary event left an indelible mark on my sister's life, haunting her regularly.

After the war my Uncle Yesheya claimed that without a wife and daughters he didn't know how to care for a child, and asked my mother to keep Irwin, who had survived most of the war with us. Irwin was my first cousin, who was an adopted brother. During the three years under Nazi occupation, we never cried. We knew that our tears would only cause anguish for our parents who could not do anything more than they were already doing to try and save us. But at the moment of liberation we not only cried, we screamed with joy. However, we did not rush to leave the forest. Frankly, we didn't know where to go. Toward the end of the war, local partisans were in Kobylnik. Believing that the Jewish families did not survive, they decided to burn down their homes. They didn't want anyone else living in them. Our house was of course among those burned down. We later heard an eyewitness account of the burning incident. The forest dugouts were our home for the past 20 months. We had almost forgotten what it was like to live in a house.

The next day we decided to leave the forest. We moved in the direction of our town. As we neared Kobylnik, we stopped to rest awhile near an old farmhouse. As we sat there resting a woman came out of the house and looked at us strangely.

She walked toward us and when she got close enough, she examined my mother and asked, "Is that you Chavkah? Where are you going looking like a beggar? The people in your village will laugh and rejoice seeing you this way. Come into my house."

The woman led mother into her bedroom and picked out one of her own dresses and told mother to put it on. "I want you to enter your village with pride. You deserve it."

This deed still brings a tear to my eyes, as it is difficult for one to comprehend the sacrifice this woman made by giving up one of her very few dresses to my mother. It was this type of kindness that restored our faith in humanity.

After this stop, we were about one mile away from our hometown. We did not hurry. We were filled with anxiety and fear of the unknown. We heard rumors that in some towns the few returning Jews were met with hostility and some were even killed when they requested the return of what they left with Christians for safekeeping before the war.

We entered our home village that now looked like a ghost town. Half of it was burned down by the partisans. There wasn't a living soul in sight. We walked through the marketplace and down to our street. Even our chimney was dismantled, for the bricks others could use. When we crossed the bridge looking for a place to stop, an elderly lady came out and invited us in. My parents knew her. Old lady Jalubowski.

She was an old friend of my grandmother, Rivka. Her house was very modest with one large room, a small kitchen, and a large storage room. She told us we could stay with her until her son returned from Germany. (After the Kobylnik Jews were killed, the Germans grabbed young Christian people, men, and women, and sent them to Germany for slave labor.) She had only one extra bed where her son had slept. Like our old modest home in Kobylnik, she had a brick oven that was built in the middle of the kitchen taking up almost a quarter of that room. My parents and Sheldon slept on the backside brick elevation off that oven. Sheldon was now three years old and had absolutely no memory of us living in any house. The one extra bed served all four children (me, Mina, Joshua, and Irwin). The four of us could fit in the one bed by lying perpendicular to how one person would sleep, like sardines. When nighttime came, we laid down in the bed trying to get comfortable, but none of us could fall asleep. In quick succession we climbed out of the bed and laid down on the floor. There we slept like babies. As for my two older brothers who were not with us, we assumed that they didn't survive the war.

Also, a couple of days after we arrived back to Kobylnik from the forest a young German soldier showed up in our marketplace. This soldier was very young and appeared to have just finished high school. My father later told us that the soldier's age was a sign that the Germans must be in trouble. Evidently, he was left behind in the forest. Hunger and thirst brought him to our town. The Jews started to gather around him and talked of killing him.

My father approached and broke up the angry crowd and told them, "Don't anybody put a finger on him. He is a prisoner of war. We must turn him over to the Russian army."

One of the men shouted, "The Russians will kill him the way the Germans killed the Russian prisoners of war."

"We don't know that for sure, and that will be their responsibility," father responded.

He gave the young German soldier some water to drink and something to eat and told him, "We are Jews. We don't kill innocent people."

We turned him over to the Russian soldiers when they were coming through our town on the way to the front lines. We had no idea what happened to him. Along with my siblings, I felt great pride in my father's actions. He taught us an important lesson at a young age which stayed with us all our lifetimes.

At this point, each child was responsible for finding food. We didn't have anything to pay in exchange, but my father had many friends in the nearby villages, and they helped us. They frequently gave us some free produce.

Lady Jalubowski took a liking to me and taught me how to brush out her angora rabbits and then spin the fur into thread. This was a marvel to me, and I did it almost weekly as the fur continued to be produced by those sweet rabbits.

It is hard to remember everything that happened in the following few weeks when we remained in our town with old lady Jalubowski after emerging from the forest. One thing, however, remains seared in my memory. A man came by to notify us that there was a letter addressed to the Swirski family at the post office. My father ran there and opened the letter looking first and only at the signature of my oldest brother, Meyer. Father immediately called my mother from the post office and hearing that her oldest son was alive, Mother promptly fainted. The overwhelming joy of knowing that one of the lost brothers was still alive revived happiness in our hearts.

My brother Hertzel's fate was traced back after the war. On the night of the final solution, when the situation seemed hopeless, Hertzel, two years older than me, asked for permission to run. My parents agreed and he ran with a friend to a neighboring town, which had already been set up as a ghetto. When we were in the Miadel ghetto, we encountered people we knew who saw him there. The Nazis gave those people a choice whether to go to Kovne or Vilna. Hertzel chose Vilna because we had relatives there. He did not know they were already all dead. Those that signed up for Vilna were taken to Panary by train. We believed this was the only time that Jews rebelled. Planning an attack with only knives as a weapon, when they arrived to Panary and the cattle-car doors were opened, squinting to adjust to sunlight, those young people jumped off and attacked the Lithuanian policemen, trying to kill as many as they could. Of course, those brave souls were shot dead, but others jumped from the train and tried to run away. Knowing my brother's spirit, I believe he was one of those that jumped and ran. At this point one of two things could have happened: like many others he could have been shot running away, or taken to Panary, where they took groups of 10 at a time to be shot at the edge of a ditch and left to die if they didn't die instantly. After the war, I could not rest until I inquired with people who saw him and traced his whereabouts. We are certain that his life ended in Panary.

Just a couple of weeks after we first escaped into the forest, starving and deprived of almost all human needs, we had a small chance to bribe a local farmer who agreed to travel to that ghetto with an extra set of farmer's clothes for Hertzel and try to bring him out. Mother was all for it, but Father hesitated. "Is it better to die by being shot, or slowly die of hunger?" He didn't want to bring Hertzel into our miserable situation, hoping that wherever he was, perhaps he escaped or even died a swift and painless death. Although we always hoped we might live, the odds were against us. When we were liberated, I understood this decision haunted my father. My mother never brought it up with him again.

Though military actions were still raging beyond our location, the Russians opened a school right away in Kobylnik. I went gladly to school to see what I still remembered at the age of 13. I remember a profound feeling of loneliness and sadness that I was the only Jewish child in my whole class. In school I did meet a few girls I knew before the war. Since I had no books, I asked one of the girls if I could come over to her house to do homework with her. She agreed. When I walked through their front door her parents looked at me with disgust, probably because I was dressed in awful hand-me-down clothes. We sat down in the girl's bedroom preparing to do homework when through a crack in her open closet I noticed one of my old dresses hanging there. My mother's cousin from Hodutishki (Adutishki) had crocheted that dress for me. It was one-of-a-kind. I was the only person to have a dress like that and the shock of seeing it hanging in her closet caused me to gasp.

Without thinking I spoke out, "That is my dress."

The girl turned sharply to me and asked slowly with anger, "Did you give it to me?"

I said, "No."

She replied, "The Germans gave it to me, and now it is mine!"

I didn't say another word about it, but I did tell my parents the story when I returned home. Because of my father's kind and gentle nature, he tried to console me by saying, "It would be too small for you now anyway. Someday you will have nicer dresses."

A few days after the dress incident, I recall two more Jewish families returned to our town. We exchanged stories of our survival. One young man came from a nearby town. His last name was also Swirski. Someone had told him that a Swirski survived in Kobylnik, and he was hoping we were his family. We were not related. I remember that only then, when the feeling of danger was slowly replaced with something resembling safety, did we begin to feel the terrible pain of our enormous loss.

18

Postavy

We heard that some of the other Jews who survived by hiding in the forest or fought with the partisans were congregating in a much larger town nearby, called Postavy. My parents decided we would leave our town for good. We said goodbye with sincere gratitude to old lady Jalubowski who hosted us after fleeing the forest. We had no luggage. The clothes on our backs were all we possessed. My father stopped a military truck and asked the driver if he was going to Postavy. He said, "yes," and gladly gave us a ride. The whole family hopped on the truck and again we ventured into the unknown. I was glad to physically leave, because our pain and sadness of all we had lost, along with the graves of those we loved dearly, were too much to bear. Because we had no childhood home left, we sensed we might never see this place again.

We arrived in Postavy and immediately found a place to live with another Jewish family whose house had not been destroyed. They also recently emerged from the forest where we all survived. I had never seen houses this big. Without the threat of danger these ample accommodations gave me the feeling of normalcy, a feeling long forgotten. My father found a job right away, which meant we would have food to eat. At that time our food consisted of mostly bread, cabbage and eggs. I will never forget that bread. It was milled with the outer wheat husk and even after baking it would cause us to choke.

My nightmares started shortly after liberation. They started in Postavy after the war and lasted for a few years. (I don't remember dreaming in the forest, but then again, our sleep was highly erratic as the conditions were awful.) The nightmare was always the same: we were in a forest and the Germans were chasing us with dogs. We were trying to escape but we were paralyzed with fear and knee deep in snow. Each time I would wake up sweating and screaming. If my parents heard me, they would try to calm me down. As was customary in the old country, to ward off bad spirits my mother would turn her head and figuratively spit three times ("poo-poo-poo").

We learned that school had just resumed so we went to register and determine our grade placement. I told the teachers that I was willing to work hard in order to catch up with my grade level. Russian grammar and math were among the subjects I had to relearn. All four of us took to learning with great enthusiasm. Even though we didn't have enough paper to write on, within one month we were promoted to the next higher grade. Even so, we were still a year older than the other kids. My younger brother, Joshua, was a math whiz. If I ever failed to understand something, he was always willing to help me out.

Every month the school principal posted on a bulletin board the names of the best students. The grading system was numeric: 5 was excellent; 4 was very good; 3 was average; 2 or

1 were failing grades. Seriously applying myself, I succeeded in not having anything lower than a 4. I earned only one 4 and that was in gymnastics. I made friends easily. In literature we had to memorize poems by heart. It was not easy since Russian was not my first language. I tried hard and succeeded. Even today I remember by heart the poetry by Pushkin, Lermontov, and Nekrasov. There were only six Jewish children in the whole school, and we all hung out together.

As a teenager, after school, I babysat for a young Jewish boy. The boy's mother gave me money to take him to the movies so that she could go out and flirt with the officers who were housed in a special military community. Russian movies were something I had never experienced. The little boy would fall asleep, and I would sit with quiet anticipation to watch the movie, twice. I memorized the songs from the movie and had a good time singing them in school. This marked the beginning of a new life for me. I was in that Postavy school for two years between the ages of 13-15. I met there a young Jewish girl from Russia; she was a survivor of the Leningrad blockade. Her name was Maya, and she became my lifelong friend. She passed away a few years ago. I am still in touch with her daughter and granddaughter.

During that time my father managed a warehouse where the farmers deposited their goods that had been requested by the government. On occasion they would bring extra produce that they sold to us. We did not go hungry in Postavy.

News that allied forces had defeated Germany soon arrived in Postavy. News reels showed images of German officers coming out of the bunkers with white flags in their hands. Alongside those reports were images of concentration camps being liberated. No word was mentioned that those skeletal bodies were Jews.

One day a request came for my father to be a witness in a trial for another man from Kobylnik. Apparently, he was found in the city of Vilna hiding under an assumed name. It was the mayor who collaborated with the Germans.

The judge asked my father, "What was his crime?"

My father said, "He helped the Germans kill the Jews in my town."

The judge asked my father again, "Besides killing Jews, is there anything else he has done?"

My father said, "Yes, he also helped kill all the communists."

The judge said, "Now that is a different story," and sentenced the mayor to fifteen years in Siberia.

My father returned home very disappointed in the Russian system of justice. Killing Jews was not a crime. Shortly thereafter, we learned that the Soviets were allowing all former Polish citizens to return to Poland. My father was the first one to sign up to do so. He also urged all the Jews who had lived in our area to do the same. While we were waiting for our turn to leave Russia, we were considered traitors. It was during that time period a stranger showed up at our house. We were sitting around the table eating and talking when he walked into the room. We all looked up at him not knowing who he was.

My mother asked, "How can we help you?"

As the stranger took off his hat, our baby brother (who was in the bedroom peeking out and had never seen him before) screamed "Meyer!"

In disbelief my mother leaned in searching for a mark on his forehead where Meyer had been kicked by a horse in childhood. When she saw the mark, she fainted.

This was an indescribable joy for the whole family. He had changed so dramatically since he left home as a 15-year-old boy that we could not recognize him. He told us he was sent to a work camp along with our cousin, Michel Patashnik.

When they heard a rumor that the German soldiers were gathering in a nearby town to kill all the Jews in our area, Michel told Meyer, "You are coming with me!"

My brother, Meyer was only 15 years old. However, Michel Patashnik had already finished serving the Polish army in the previous war and witnessed firsthand, in the middle of the night, the massacre of all the Jews from his town of Hodutishki (Adutishki). He was not going to wait for it to happen again. Michel and Meyer, and a small group of privy men, ran to the forest and wandered around there for almost three months. They had nothing and did not know where they were going. The two of them were freezing and starving.

Michel eventually came up with a plan. His army experience taught him that a frontline is not always well guarded. If they could make it to the frontline, they would find a way to cross into Russia. They lay on the ground for days in a nearby forest watching the German patrols move and travel toward the frontline. They had to time it just right. The first attempt was made by my brother, Meyer. He ran in the middle of the night past the frontline and reached the first house he found. The woman who answered the door welcomed him in. Michel tried the next night and he too made it across. My brother was sent to work in a *kolchoz* (Russian collective farm) and our cousin, Michel (a man already of age) was mobilized in the Russian army.

Eventually, when he reached the age of 16, my brother, Meyer, was sent to work in Stalingrad in a factory where they produced tanks. When he showed up at our door in Postavy in

1946, he had come directly from Stalingrad. Since our family was already planning to leave Russia soon, Father told Meyer he should do the same. Father approached a Polish man with a typical Polish name, who was scheduled to leave for Poland with the next transport and offered to buy his identification papers.

"You can tell the authorities that you lost them, and they will issue you new documents." The man agreed for a price.

As soon as my brother took off for Poland, my father went and bought a one-way ticket to Stalingrad. This was done so that if there was an inquiry, he would have proof that Meyer went back on a specific date. To make the ploy complete, a few weeks later he wrote and sent a letter to Meyer's Stalingrad address asking whether he was well and wondering why the family had not yet heard from him. (At the end of the war, it was not rare that people vanished without a trace.)

We lived there for two years after liberation. For me, Postavy marked the transition from hiding in the forest toward a more conventional and new life. I had made many friends there and was sad to leave them and Postavy behind. A few months later the rest of our family left Russia for good.

19

Wandering

We arrived in Poland and soon realized that the Russians were also controlling that territory. It became a gathering place for many Holocaust survivors. Rumors were circulating that Jews who were traveling alone were being abducted and killed. We looked for a way out of Poland.

A group of young Jewish men from Palestine organized a clandestine escape route from Poland. It was called *braicha*, meaning escape. The borders at that time were not carefully guarded. Our family chose to join their organized escape. Taking only what we could carry on our backs, in the middle of the night we crossed by foot from Poland into what was then called Czechoslovakia. The group leaders put us up in rooms and allowed us a few days' rest. They told us to destroy anything written in Russian or Polish. People started to scratch out handwritten inscriptions on precious photographs. We prepared to move on.

Shortly thereafter, the same organization took us from Czechoslovakia to Vienna, Austria, this time by train. In Vienna they gave us a few months' rest. At that time as teenagers, we joined a kibbutz youth group where we were imbued with a love for Israel. Food was plentiful and they even took us to a concert and gave us some freedom to explore Vienna. It was my first real exploration of the new world. We got on a trolley car and visited world class museums. Our next stop was the American Zone in Germany. After many stops in different transit camps, they finally brought us to a place called Feldafing. That is where we finally met up with Meyer, who had arrived there a few months before us. During the war he used a different name, but at this time he changed it back to his real name, Meyer Swirski.

In Feldafing, my parents opted to put Joshua, Mina, and me into an orphanage simply because they knew the food there was better. It was in this town that I developed tonsillitis. Every swallow was accompanied by horrible pain. Mother said my tonsils looked like snowcapped mountains. I had my tonsils removed in a German hospital with my brother, Meyer, at my side. While recuperating, Meyer made sure I had plenty of pain-soothing ice cream to eat. Although our time in Feldafing was less than a year, it was eventful. Our next stop was the DP (Displaced Persons) camp, Wasseralfingen. The small town of Wasseralfingen was located near the city of Aalen. For the young adults it was an easy walk from the city to camp. If we had money, we could also hop on a bus and get there faster.

Once, while in a DP camp in Germany, a group of survivors were mingling outside when a few German children approached them begging for some food. They showed honest signs of hunger, with parched lips and sunken cheeks. Most of the encamped Jews shunned them, but when they asked my father, he took a loaf of bread and cut it into pieces and handed each child some bread.

Other people started to scold him saying, "They are German! After what the Germans did to our people you are helping them? Don't do it."

My father spoke up with restrained emotion in his voice and said, "I had to witness my own children beg for food when they were starving. I will not deny these children some food. Yes, they are German, but they are human beings."

This was an unforgettable moment. We were so full of our own emotions: pride for our father, and gratitude for this example of kindness. My siblings and I could only watch with tears in our eyes.

I must say that the DP camps were well organized. In Wasseralfingen we lived in regular houses, but they housed three families in a single-family home. My family was the largest with six people, so we got the biggest room. We all shared the kitchen.

The management of this transit camp didn't waste any time and set up schools almost immediately. This had a feel of normal life. My cousin, Irwin, was no longer with us. When we arrived in Poland, his brother, Hertzke (who just got married) took him from us. My parents stressed education above all other things. Food was provided for us by a few organizations. The largest was UNRRA (United Nations for Relief and Rehabilitation Administration). We were also aided by Jewish organizations like HIAS (Hebrew Immigration Aid Society) who distributed clothing that was donated by American Jews. Our entire wardrobe was used and donated clothing, but we didn't care. For us they were new. In this camp I was introduced to peanut butter for the first time. I loved it and ate it gladly, but most of the kids were afraid to touch an unknown item. They gave it all to me, and I started to gain weight quickly.

Because our education had been completely interrupted by the war, especially for Meyer (who was older and expected to know more), we found a professor in Aalen who agreed to help prepare Meyer for his final high school exams and diploma. I still remember the professor's name was Grosskapf. By then we started to receive food packages from my father's brother, Herman, that helped offset payments for Meyer's tutoring. I remember the highest priced consumer good we received after the war in Germany was American coffee. We didn't even know how to prepare it. It all went to Professor Grosskapf. After one year of tutoring, my brother Meyer successfully got his high school diploma.

My two younger twin siblings (Joshua and Mina) and I had a great time in our Hebrew School. A few of the teachers were emissaries from Palestine and taught us the Hebrew language and Jewish history. We took to it like fish take to water. This was all in preparation for our eventual emigration to Israel. Israel was not yet declared an independent state, but we knew that eventually it would become our homeland, and a homeland for all Jewish people. The school had dances once a month, and I was the first one to arrive and the last one to go home. We didn't have a lot of time for sports, but we played volleyball on the school playground every day. It became my favorite pastime. In other words, we resumed what many would consider a normal teenage life.

We did not want to think about the war years. We did, however, start observing a day of remembrance when our Jewish neighbors of Kobylnik were murdered by local militia and Nazi soldiers. We knew it was the day after Yom Kippur. I was about fifteen or sixteen years old, and I was overcome with emotions when I said a prayer for my brother who was murdered by the Nazis. It was numbing to remember that night and our escape, heart wrenching to think of our dear friends murdered for no reason other than their religion. I found myself crying hysterically, expressing out loud my outrage asking anyone around me, "Where was the free world? Why didn't they try to stop it? I hate all of them!" I was still so young and naive, I didn't even understand what "the free world" meant, but I had heard it referenced many times. My father heard my outburst and became concerned about my feelings of anger and hatred and asked me to sit down and talk with him.

He started the conversation with a question to me: "We were victims of hatred; did you like it?"

"Of course not."

"Then why would you do to others that which is hateful to you? The people that you hate don't know it and don't care. Your hatred will only destroy you. Try another attitude. Show kindness and caring to others, especially those who are less fortunate than you. You will be an example to others. Love and kindness can spread just as fast as hate."

His candor and wisdom forced me into introspection. I sat quietly but thought deeply about his words. My love and respect for my father had me hear his advice with an open mind and open heart. I never forgot this life-changing lesson, and I practice his advice to this day.

* * *

We were looking forward to a brighter future. I was 16 years old and suddenly became quite interested in boys. My attention was drawn to the young emissaries from the organized Israel youth groups. Unfortunately, they only met on weekends. There we learned to dance the *hora* and sing patriotic songs. The leaders of these groups always started the sessions with political speeches. I enjoyed every moment of it, and so did many of my friends. We also started to make friends with German families and started to copy their customs. We began to follow their custom of a pitcher of beer with lunch. It was good fun.

The highlight of that time was the news from Israel. In the United Nations they were about to take up the issue of declaring Israel as a sovereign state and admitting it to the United Nations. We were glued to the radio listening to the news. On the day the vote came up, we sat with paper and pencil tallying every vote. We were excited and concerned about the outcome. Most importantly we waited anxiously for the American vote. When America finally voted "yes," we danced for joy. It was May 11, 1948.

Our youth group leaders, together with the school, organized a midnight march through the town. They gave us Israeli flags and lit torches as we started to march. First, we sang the Hatikva (Israeli's national anthem) followed by any Hebrew song we knew. We danced the *hora* on the corner of every new street. Even without the beer, we were drunk with joy. In that moment, I remember thinking it was easy to realize the most important events in my life up until that time: (1) liberation one year before the war ended; (2) Germany's surrender; and (3) the creation of the state of Israel.

My brother, Meyer, had already started studying at the university in Shtutgart. He came home and told our parents that Israel is fighting for its existence. "I must go and help fight the war." My father gave him his blessings and along with another youth, Meyer was transported to Israel. It was called *gius* (a free-will mobilization). I also felt that I could be of some help there. I was seventeen years old and imbued with the spirit of Zionism. We had endured WWII, and the Jewish people were finally going to have a homeland of their own. I wanted to go. But it was 1948 and my parents' mentality was typical for that generation. They would not allow a girl to fight when they knew it was dangerous. Of lesser importance a woman traveling without an escort was still socially unacceptable. I was very disappointed but didn't dare to disobey my parents. The privilege to fight for Israel was not going to be mine.

Life in the DP camps went on as usual. In addition to our regular schoolwork, my father thought it would be a good idea that I start taking private lessons with my brother's tutor, Professor Grosskopf, to prepare for a high school diploma. I enjoyed the lessons in physics, mathematics, and the German language. Between academic lessons we often discussed politics and what it was like for a German opposing Hitler to survive under the Nazi regime. A transgression as small as listening to the BBC on the radio could cost a person a job, or even worse, to be classified as an enemy of the Reich. He explained to me that not every German supported Hitler even if they were forced to join the Nazi party to keep their jobs. It was clear he was speaking of himself.

After three years in the displaced persons camp, people started to look for possibilities to leave Germany. Many went to Israel. Our original intention was to do the same. We received a letter from Meyer who had just been discharged from the Israeli army. He described how he was accepted to the Haifa Technion to study engineering. Life in Israel was very difficult immediately after the War of Independence, and if we were to go then he would have had to quit school to help support the family. He suggested that it might be a good idea for us to go to the United States of America, where we had very close family, and then come to Israel a few years later. We immediately applied for visas to the United States. Everyone was x-rayed before coming to the American consulate. Because of a blemish on Father's lung x-ray, we were rejected without recourse. We could go to Australia because they accepted everyone. That was much too far from Israel and from our two uncles who lived in the United States.

All the smaller DP camps started to empty out and those who were left in remote places were consolidated and sent to the larger Wasseralfingen camp where we remained. Some of the new residents we knew from before the war, and others were total strangers. Among those we did know was a family from a small town in Poland, not far from ours; I knew the town of Adutishki because before the war I spent a few summer breaks there with my aunt. The family had two sons. One was my age and an avid volleyball player, with whom I played on the same team. The older son, Ed, was a student at Erlongen University. Although Ed was a student, when he had time off during the summer, he came back to Wasseralfingen to visit his parents. He had no interest in playing volleyball with us. On occasion he would come by our house with the pretext of discussing politics with my father, but we all understood his real motive being in our home. To be polite I served them tea and then quietly went out to play volleyball with my team. I saw how Ed's eyes followed my every move.

It was around this time I became very sick with terrible abdominal pains and a high fever. My mother tried desperately to find a remedy for me, but nothing worked. They finally called the DP camp's doctor who made a house call. He came in, looked at my stomach, pressed it and made a quick diagnosis of appendicitis. He urged my parents to rush me to the hospital in Aalen because he believed my appendix was on the verge of bursting. In pain and scared, I was anxious about being treated by a German doctor in a German hospital. To quell my concerns my parents asked a Jewish nurse to accompany me. The operation was a success, though I did have to spend a whole week in the hospital. I knew my parents would never leave me behind but lying there I allowed myself to imagine the camp being dismantled and them being forced to leave without me. On my last day there, a nurse came in and told me that I had a visitor. The Jaffe's older son, Ed (then known as Ephraim), walked in to see me. I was taken by complete surprise. He told me he had been in the hospital visiting his father, and when he realized I was in that same hospital he decided to look in on me. We had a nice conversation and he assured me that the camp was still there. Years later, when Ed became my husband, he told me that during that visit he realized how beautiful I was.

Rumors started to circulate that Wasseralfingen would soon merge with another camp. As more and more people emigrated, the camp was in fact closing. We faced an uncertain future not knowing which country would let us in.

They took us by train to our next stop, Funkenkasserne, a DP camp right outside of Shtutgart. There we found refugees from many different places. The loudspeaker constantly played English songs on a loop. We learned the songs by heart quickly and sang happily *You Are My Sunshine*, and *My Bonnie Lies Over the Ocean*, among others. This was the beginning of our English language acquisition. They also offered English classes and we took them gladly. It was nice to learn something useful. They also had dances for the young people, that my siblings and I attended regularly. In this camp there were many Armenians who spoke Russian, so we had a common language. They had escaped from Russia and were looking to emigrate to the United States. We became good friends and spent a lot of time together. The Armenians were in this camp for a long while. They showed us how to get on a streetcar that would take us to the center of Shtutgart. In Shtutgart we could see a movie or get cheap tickets to the opera (standing room only), and we began to absorb the German culture. All we really cared about at the time was to enjoy ourselves.

After a few months at Funkenkasserne they shipped us to a camp called Boblingen. Here too we found refugees of all different nationalities. It was a large camp and we mingled on the volleyball court and near the kiosk where I was introduced to an American drink called Coca-Cola for the very first time. The Jaffe family also moved from camp to camp with us and it was Ed who offered me the first Coke I ever drank. I must say that I didn't care for it much, but I pretended to like it.

In this camp I met a Russian man with whom I often had political discussions. He explained to me how the Russian system operates. I was shocked to learn how the NKVD secret service—now also known as the KGB—would show up in the middle of the night, arrest people and take them to the *gulag* prisons and they were never seen again. Among other reasons, he explained clearly this was why he didn't ever want to return to the Soviet Union, and like us was looking for a country where he could start a new life.

In Boblingen, the Jaffe family got their visas to emigrate to the United States. We said goodbye to them, and we started to look for other possibilities.

From Boblingen they shipped us to the largest DP camp that was still functioning called Foehrenwald, not far from Munich. There we stayed for almost a full year. My younger siblings started school again. With my newfound English and typing skills I landed a paying job in the administrative offices filling out documents for people applying to emigrate to Australia. It was hard not to notice how other girls appeared: wearing make-up, red nail polish, and fancy hairdos. I followed suit, because I was 19 years old, and just looking to have a good time.

The office manager there was a middle-aged man. He acquired a law degree before the war and was well respected by everyone. One day the office manager asked me into his office and told me he wanted to give me some advice.

"You seem different from the other girls. You are attractive without the makeup; you don't need red nail polish and fancy hairdos. Intelligent boys will like you for who you are, and not for who you are trying to be."

It gave me pause, especially because everyone respected him so much, including me. I mulled over his advice and decided to take it, which also delighted my parents. They had been reluctant to say anything to me, fearing I would call them "old fashioned." I never forgot that moment and his lesson.

Our next best chance was Canada. Some of our old friends who emigrated to Canada about a year ago wrote and sent us affidavits with a guarantee for work and lodging. The greatest hurdle was the Canadian ministry, which had the reputation of rejecting most Jews. When our turn came and we walked in before the Council, I recognized his interpreter. It was a young Ukrainian man who had been in my English classes. When the Canadian official asked a question, the so-called interpreter was twisting the answer. Nervous and annoyed, I jumped in and responded with my nascent English. The official was impressed and decided to address his questions to me directly. I answered the best I could, and he kept smiling. He asked how come Mina and Joshua were born on the same date.

I told him, "They are twice."

He corrected me and said the word is "twins."

Then he asked me, "What will you do in Canada?"

I told him, "I am a good seamstress. I even know how to make patterns."

I believe he liked my self-confidence. He stamped our visas and wished us good luck. When we walked out, the people next in line were pleasantly surprised that we were approved.

Leaning in I told them, "The problem is the interpreter, not the official."

Waiting for our departure, we spent about two months in Bremerhaven. We explored the city and met other refugees who were waiting for a boat to take us to Canada. English and typing classes were offered almost daily, and I took them. But in the evenings, we went to German nightclubs and danced till dawn.

One evening we were joined by a young man who was kind of short and a bit on the chubby side. I watched as he asked a few of the girls to dance and they all declined. I felt sorry for him, so when he came over and asked me, I got up to dance with him. Well, it turned out that he was a professional dancer, and together we dominated the dance floor for the rest of the evening. It was very easy to follow him, and I had a great time that evening. You know what they say: don't judge a book by its cover.

Although we were managing to keep ourselves busy, we knew this was only one stop along our journey. Finally, our boat arrived at the harbor. It was called the *Anna Salen*. It had been used during the war for carrying cargo and transporting soldiers. Ships of this kind were dubbed "Liberty Ships." They put us in steerage on the lowest level of the ship; we had no choice in the matter. Our beds were hanging hammocks. Men were lodged one level above us with the same accommodations. Mealtime was when we all met in the dining room. We knew that we, and a few people traveling with us, were the lucky ones. We were leaving Europe behind us, with all the pain and sadness of WWII.

With the exception of my oldest brother, Meyer, who was already in Israel studying engineering at Haifa's Technion University, the most important thing for us was traveling together as a family. There were very few families who survived with both parents and siblings. I was 20 years old; the twins (Mina and Joshua) were 18, and Sheldon (born 10 days before Nazi Germany attacked the Soviet Union) was already 10 years old.

During the DP camp years, we learned that the German government was paying restitution to survivors for our suffering under the Nazi regime. With that one-time payout my parents decided to buy a pair of silver candlestick holders, a Doxa watch, and a set of Rosenthal dishes. The candlestick holders represented the significance of the Jewish tradition of lighting candles on Friday nights. The watch and dishes were thought to be so valuable we might benefit from them in the new world. Those few items were joined with a few other small items given to us by our American relatives. We didn't have much of anything else.

20

The Voyage to Canada

The first day on the boat was glorious. Despite our strict kosher diet, there was an abundance of food to eat. Dairy products were plentiful along with fish, herring, and all the bread and butter we could eat!

The women's lowest level compartments housed approximately 20 women. One bathroom served us all so the line was always long. I learned not to wait until the urge struck to get in line. There were inconveniences, but my sister and I got plenty of attention from the young men on board.

Departing Germany our boat had not been stocked fully with all the provisions we needed for the voyage, so we made a stop in Holland to pick up cheese, fresh fruit and more. While we remained close to the European continent, we all felt great. However, only one day later when we entered the vastness of the Atlantic Ocean, immediately after breakfast my mother, Mina and I all fell ill with sea sickness. It was horrible. Mother was afflicted most, so much so that

Mina and I had to carry her out on the deck where she could breathe fresh air. The only thing she could tolerate eating was a piece of herring and dry crusty bread. Feeling the way we did, we decided to stay up on deck and ultimately slept wherever we found a corner to curl up and put our heads down.

About a day or two before we reached the port city of Halifax, Canada, the stormy weather subsided and we were feeling better. Someone had a camera and took a picture of me, my sister, and another young man that we met on the boat. Since our future was very uncertain, we didn't even bother writing down the young man's name so he would remain a stranger. But it felt great to see the shores of Canada. I promised myself that I would never get on a boat again.

That boat journey took almost two weeks to reach the shores of Canada. Sea sickness aside, Mina was also very sick with menstrual bleeding and the authorities decided that she must be hospitalized right away. Trains were on stand-by to take the boat immigrants to Toronto. My parents had to make a quick decision that I should stay in Halifax with Mina until she was well. I found myself on that train getting instructions from my parents on what to do and how to stay in touch with them when we heard an announcement come over the loudspeaker of the train.

"Someone is looking for the Swirski family."

We thought it must be our cousin, Irwin who left for Canada two years before us and heard we were arriving and came to greet us. We looked for him but could not find him. It turned out that the young man looking for the Swirski family was someone we did not know. He lived in Halifax and was actively seeking a bride. He proactively read the ship's passenger list where he noticed a Jewish family with two single daughters arriving. He wanted to meet us. Little did he know these two single ladies would be staying in Halifax for a few weeks.

My parents and brothers left on that train for Toronto. My sister was taken straight to the hospital, and I was assigned bed accommodations in a refugee hall across town. The young man from the train was a modern orthodox Jew named Phil Shenker. His parents owned a bakery where he also worked. He turned out to be a godsend for me. The few weeks that I stayed in Halifax he gave me his close attention. He showed me around town, introduced me to a few prominent Jewish families who all invited me over for lunch, and Phil would take me out to dinner several times a week. I visited my sister in the hospital every day and when the time came to depart for Toronto and rejoin my parents, I was sad to leave this beautiful city behind me. Phil kept corresponding with me until he learned I got married.

By the time Mina and I arrived in Toronto my father had landed a job that came with a small apartment, as part of his renumeration. He was the caretaker of a conservative synagogue and was paid $5 a week. The one-bedroom apartment was in the back of the synagogue. My parents got the bedroom, and the living room was converted at night into a bedroom for us three young adults and one child. Members of that synagogue gave us two pullout sofas that became our beds. The kitchen was small, but my mother always found room for a guest or two. Despite the confined space, we were happy finally to have a place of our own. The first task at hand was to find jobs for the three adult children. Sheldon enrolled in third grade. At 10 years of age, he was totally undisciplined and had no interest in learning. We received teacher complaints about his behavior every day.

I started work in a coat factory as a seamstress. That first week I earned $15. After a short period of observation, the supervisor told me I was not well suited to the job and offered me the position of coat examiner for $25 a week. I gladly accepted.

Our evenings were filled with night school learning English. In fact, I went straight from work to school and ate dinner afterwards. For me school was a great deal of fun. It was social, and I met other newcomers from different countries. I even recognized a few people from the DP camps in Germany.

All three of us worked and we gave everything we earned to my mother who ran the household. The hardest part was in the morning, when all three of us needed to rush out to work and we had to share one bathroom. Aside from that, we were young and happy to be in Canada, which was very close to the United States.

My father's brother lived in Brooklyn, New York. Uncle Herman traveled to Toronto to visit us. Having not seen each other for 20 years, it was a very emotional reunion. They hardly recognized one another. This meeting made us wish for nothing more than to be reunited on a permanent basis.

As soon as my English improved enough, I started looking for a better job. I was trained as a bookkeeper in Europe, and I was also good on a typewriter. I found a job listing for an office position with a publishing company. I interviewed and got the job. Life was looking up for me. There were Saturday night stag dance parties at one of the larger synagogues. I was glad to attend with or without a date. I always had a good time and even met a few interesting people. By this time my English had improved enough that I stopped night school. Instead, I used my evenings to enroll in a night school for budding Hebrew school teachers. It was a serious school called Hertzeliya. I was certain this made my father very proud of me. After everything we had been through, it was important to me to please both my parents. For example, if

I met and started dating a guy my parents didn't like, I felt I could no longer see him.

It was around this time I got a phone call from Ed Jaffe whom I had met in Wasseralfingen. He wanted to know if I was dating anyone seriously. I said no. Then he asked if I would like a visit from him. I told him, "Gladly." We had known each other from the same region, and he was an interesting man; though here again I was influenced by my parents who guided me toward a smart and well-educated man, which made Ed a real catch.

21

Edward Ephraim Jaffe

A couple of weeks later I met Ed at the bus station in Toronto. I could not understand why he was wearing a hat. When I asked him why, he told me that he didn't want to shock me. During the last two years that we did not see one another he had lost most of his hair. It must have been very hard on a 24-year-old man. I assured him that what mattered most to me was the person, not his hair. At the time, I imagined he lost his hair from either or both anxiety or the stress of handling a full-time day job and going to City College at night taking full time course credits. All in all, his visit was a success. He promised to come back as soon as he could.

At the same time, my sister Mina started dating a young man from the United States who already owned a car. He suggested to Ed that they travel together on the next journey up to Toronto. A companion would be welcome, and they could share the expenses. Mina married Nathan Kasdan only a few months after they started dating. Among newcomers this was not unusual. We had missed out on so much life during the war, it felt like there was no time to waste. On the other hand, my engagement lasted almost a year. Ed explained that he wanted to complete his master's degree in Organic Chemistry before we got married. An engagement ring on my finger kept other men from pursuing me. The timing turned out to be perfect because I was needed at home. My mother discovered a lump in her breast that turned out to be cancer. The breast was removed, and I accompanied her to all her daily radiation treatments. My father was devastated, and it was the first time I saw my father cry. Whether coincidental or not, it was at this time my father's health began to deteriorate. I had to go grocery shopping with him, and he would sometimes have such strong chest pains we would stop, and he put nitroglycerin under his tongue. I took him to a heart specialist who told me that there was nothing he could do for him. He suggested that father live his life without restrictions.

Ed visited as often as he could. But because I could not become an American citizen until I married him, we had a civil ceremony first. After Ed received his master's degree, we had a Jewish ceremony and party in Toronto on July 4th, 1954. July 4th was also the day we were liberated. Ed explained that it was a holiday in the United States and attending a wedding on a holiday made everything easier for our family and friends. To this very day, July 4th remains a very special day for me in more ways than one!

My cousin Remmy Safran suggested we take a honeymoon to an inexpensive cottage set behind a roadside inn. We didn't have a car, so he volunteered to drop us off there and come back in a week to bring us home. Having absolutely no experience in matters of this sort, we agreed. It turned out to be a bad decision as there was no place within walking distance to go, and the food, which was passable, was the same every single day. I was bored and unhappy but embarrassed to complain or even dream of calling a cab to take us home. When the week was up, Remmy drove us to my parents' home where I packed my few belongings and days later Ed and I took a train from Toronto to New York City.

Ed had not yet arranged for a separate apartment for us, so we were forced to live a few weeks with his parents in Manhattan. I knew immediately that we needed to find a place of our own because their apartment was very small and dark, with only one window.

While still living with Ed's parents, one month after our wedding, news arrived that my father had a massive heart attack and died in bed earlier that day. He had gotten up to bring in the milk bottles left outside on the porch but was feeling funny, so he decided to go back to bed and didn't get up. I knew his heart was vulnerable, but this news hit me hard, as Father was the backbone of our family and was adored by us all for his wisdom, affection, and goodness. Mina and I took a train back to Toronto for the funeral. We remained there for a week observing *shiva*, a period of mourning, with my other family members. I was heartbroken.

Meanwhile Ed found an apartment for us and two weeks later we moved into the third-floor walk up at St. John's Place near Eastern Parkway. This was a very positive development, as not only did I have a place where I could feel at home, but a distant cousin of mine, Helen Hershkowitz, lived on that very same block. Ed resumed his doctoral studies which required long and late hours at the University. During that period, I spent quite a bit of time at my cousin's house and learned a great deal from her. I found a bookkeeper's job in Manhattan which paid enough to cover all our rent, food, and subway fares. Helen Hershkowitz was a lifesaver for me. I was still so green around the edges, and she lovingly explained things to me. I stayed in touch with her daughter, for whom I babysat, and decades later her son, Alan, who was born after we moved away, came to visit me with tales of his life and the book he wrote discovering how his father survived a concentration camp during the war.

22

Building a Family

Ed completed his PhD three years later. I typed his thesis using an old-fashioned typewriter. I remember it being excruciatingly difficult, but I managed to get through it because I was now living for two, pregnant with my first child! Rebecca was born in Brooklyn on August 15, 1957, and named, of course, for my beloved Grandmother, Rivka. We bought a beautiful baby carriage so that I could walk her in Prospect Park, where all the young mothers used to congregate. I could not possibly carry the baby carriage up three floors to our apartment, so I looked around in the basement of our building to see if there might be a place to store it. There I found a gentleman who was the maintenance man for our building. He was very friendly and soon we were talking like old friends. As we moved about the basement together, I realized that he was sleeping there on a mattress on the floor, with evidence of empty bean cans. Feeling free to do so, I asked him why he stayed down there and ate only beans, and he quickly replied with wide eyes that he was glad to have a warm place to sleep and that beans were full of protein and very inexpensive. He suddenly seemed worried and asked me not to tell anyone that we spoke, for fear of losing his job. His fear of talking with a white woman, because of possible repercussions, made it clear to me that he would not be treated fairly, perhaps because of the color of his skin. This was my first personal encounter with what I believed was the result of discrimination and inequality in this country.

Ed was highly recommended by his thesis professors, Morrison and Boyd. This is one of the reasons that he was hired quickly by the DuPont Company right on campus. This meant we would have to move from Brooklyn to New Jersey, and after three years living in that walk-up apartment, I was overjoyed to move on. More importantly to me was that my mother and Sheldon had moved to Elizabeth, New Jersey, where she got a job working for their orthodox Jewish community. Her job did not pay much, but it also came with an apartment, so she was able to enroll Sheldon in an orthodox Jewish high school in New York City.

Our first New Jersey apartment was in Newark, because Ed reported to DuPont's Newark laboratory. We rented a place at The Ivy Hill Apartments. Ed was a diligent and ambitious chemist. With dedication and hard work, he quickly made a name for himself and felt comfortable in the lab. Separately, my job was to learn about motherhood. I purchased Dr. Spock's popular book *Baby and Child Care* and referenced it daily. It answered all my questions and I raised Rebecca by that book. Walking our children, young mothers like myself met in the park every day, and I made friends. As a couple our main goal was to save money to purchase a home of our own. We purchased our first used car and Ed learned how to drive. Now we were able to visit my mother and Ed's parents in Brooklyn. We were extremely happy to be mobile and close to family.

Rebecca learned quickly and dazzled bystanders by clearly reciting the entire alphabet at the age of two. With savings and Ed's job, I started to seek out affordable homes in the area. A friend took me to see new split-level homes being built in Union, New Jersey. I was very interested and chatted with the sales representative on price and loans. Once again, I was such a novice, I had no idea whether we could afford such a home or not. But when I told her how much savings we had and Ed's salary, she said, "People are buying these homes with much less! You can do it."

After two years in Newark, New Jersey, we moved to our first new house. It was easy to make new friends because all the people on our street were also new homeowners with young children. It was time to grow our family. Our daughter, Linda Sue, was born August 29, 1960. We were overjoyed having two beautiful, healthy girls.

As the girls were growing up and I became an efficient homemaker, I found that I had a little free time. I explored the possibility of finishing my studies for a Hebrew School Teacher's Certificate. The Midrasha in West Orange was accepting students with a solid Jewish background. I applied and took tests in Hebrew and Jewish History. They gave me full credit for both subjects. Because many of the students in that Midrasha were mothers with young children, most classes took place on Sunday evening. Ed took care of the children while I was out at school. At that time there was a shortage of Hebrew School teachers, so I was able to start teaching part-time before I received all my credits.

Our son, David Lawrence, was born August 13, 1964, four years after Linda. Blessed with another healthy child, Ed was overjoyed with his new son.

While Ed advanced well at work, I took care of the house, the children, my studies, and our social life. We could now afford a new car and the first was a Chevrolet. Until then I had not driven, but soon I got my license to drive and thereafter drove the girls to school. Eventually I got a car of my own. Most of my family lived nearby and this was an enormous comfort to me. After all we had been through, I could not have wished for a better life than the 15 years we lived in our first house in Union, New Jersey.

Rebecca was an outstanding student. She was ambitious and diligent. As it turns out, when she completed 11th grade, she had accumulated enough credits to graduate from high school. Midyear she announced to us that she would be applying to college a year early and found a six-year medical program through Lehigh University. We traveled together by train to Philadelphia for her interview. I was worried that she would be disappointed if they rejected her application, especially because of her age. After the interview, I tried to read her facial expression when she returned to the waiting room, where I had remained. She admitted that it was hard to tell whether it went well, and they did ask her about her age. To distract her, I made small talk on the way home, and she told me, "If nothing else, Mom, it was a fun day traveling on the train with you, mother and daughter." She was accepted to that program and graduated with a medical degree before her 23rd birthday.

Linda had a cheerful personality and loved to dance and entertain. David was a typical boy bursting with energy and blessed with an exceptional memory. I could not have wished for anything better. Both Ed and I had survived with both sets of parents living nearby. Among immigrants like ourselves that was a rare phenomenon. In fact, my life was so good that I rarely thought about my past. That said, I reached out and offered help and moral support to other survivors because we were all newcomers to this country.

Ed worked very hard and was appreciated greatly for his advancements and discoveries in colored pigments for Du Pont. I planted trees and flowers all around our property but gave special attention to my prized rock garden which I started from scratch. There was a hill that ran the width of our property about 20 yards from the back of our house and extended to the property line. Different seasons brought different beauty among the rocks. It was a joy. I felt that working in the garden was therapeutic for both my body and soul. When things were tense at home, the earth settled me down. The attention I gave the plants almost always yielded beauty. Perhaps seeing my father plant an orchard for my mother influenced me, or maybe my love for plants is hereditary. Along with those perennials on our backyard hill, we too had finally rooted ourselves and were no longer wanderers.

We lived in that first house for fifteen years, and I remember them as the best years of my life. I was young, healthy, and full of energy, able to raise three beautiful children. My mother with my two single brothers (Joshua/ Jim and Zundel/Sheldon) as well as my sister Mina (with two daughters of her own) were a short drive away. Having my family close by for love and support made a huge difference in my daily life. In addition to my family, I made many friends and felt blessed.

In retrospect, our block seemed like a melting pot of cultures. A neighbor across the street was German; she had introduced me to her elderly mother, who had just arrived from Germany to live with her. They knew I spoke German and because her mother spoke nothing but German, she hoped we might become friendly. I had invited her mother over for a cup of tea and made small talk. This became routine and I even took her shopping and made her welcome to visit at any time. At one of these tea parties, she asked me where I was during the war. I explained I was under Nazi occupation without giving her any details.

She looked me in the eyes and confessed that her husband belonged to the Nazi party. Perhaps she felt like she had to explain and went on to say that he would not have been able to advance in the army had he not joined the Nazi party.

She continued, "I hope he didn't have to shoot any civilians. We will never know because he has been dead for some time already."

I thanked her for sharing this with me and our friendship never suffered. Sometime later she fell sick and was taken to our neighborhood hospital. I visited her there often because her daughter worked in New York City and could not get there in the middle of the day.

I can still see her face in my mind's eye because the day before she died, she told me, "Who could have thought that a Jewish woman would show me so much kindness in my last days of life."

I called her Omma, which is Grandmother in German. My friendship with Omma had made me realize that I had, in fact, overcome my hatred towards Germans despite the unimaginable pain and loss they caused the Jewish people.

Then one day my husband came home from work and announced that the Du Pont company requested he move to their headquarter city in Wilmington, Delaware. This was not unexpected because one year earlier they had proposed we try out Wilmington for a trial year, but for one year it did not make sense to move an entire family with children in school. So, Ed went to Wilmington and came home on the weekends, which worked well for everyone. Now, however, they wanted a permanent move, so we faced selling our first home and moving away. Parting from my beloved family and many friends was very difficult. We planted roots in that community, and I had invested so much energy and love into the house and garden. Even the young cherry tree I had planted myself had finally yielded fruit, though the birds ate most of the cherries before I could get to them. There was no choice; we had to pack and go.

Ed and I made a trip down to Wilmington to find a house; we settled on one that was in a good school district. Though I tried to choke back tears, I knew we were all emotional and sorry to leave Union with all that it meant to us.

23

Wilmington, Delaware

After the move and the unpacking, one of the first things on my agenda was to find a synagogue where I could feel comfortable. My first stop was in a traditional synagogue with an extremely charismatic rabbi. The search stopped there. The congregants were warm and welcoming. I quickly noticed a woman about my age who seemed to know everyone. After services she came over to say hello and asked me where I was from and where we purchased a home. When I told her, she said, "We are practically neighbors!"

Rebecca had already set off for her six-year medical program and never really spent a substantial amount of time living in the Wilmington home. Linda began high school and David went to junior high, both public schools. And I began to put my personal touch on our new home.

With some free time on my hands, I asked around about volunteering in the community. I was not yet ready to commit to a job as a Hebrew teacher. I was told there was a Jewish old age center that needed volunteers, so I went to the Kutz home and introduced myself to the residents. They asked me to read them stories to lift their spirits. For this I was ready. I chose Shalom Aleichem's funny short stories. I sensed my first time reading to them was unsuccessful because many of them fell asleep on me. I thought this was because I was not keeping eye contact with them, so I devised a plan to carefully memorize the stories by reading them beforehand, and then I would tell the stories as if they had happened to me. The third time I told the stories as if they happened to my grandmother, and with complete eye contact they became interested and even shared part of their own stories with me. We laughed together at silly circumstances, and everyone was fulfilled by the visits. I managed to return on a regular basis for an entire year.

My son David was almost bar mitzvah age, and it was time to start his Wilmington Hebrew School education. Our synagogue had an excellent school, so I arranged an interview with the school's principal, Helen Gordon. She explained that the level of Hebrew was quite high, and that David might need a tutor for a short time.

David said, "I don't need a tutor. My mother is a Hebrew school teacher. She will tutor me."

It took no time for Helen to offer me a position in their Hebrew school, and I agreed to start one day a week. Around that same time a friend told me that the Ministry of Caring needed volunteers to help prepare lunch for the poor. Having been so hungry during the war, I wanted to help and happily did so.

I had successfully integrated into this new community and made friends. One of my closest friends, Faith Brown, asked me, "Where were you during the war years?"

I had no intention of opening old wounds and talking about the war years. I thought there were other survivors who were adults during the war who could share their survival stories. I didn't want to face the old psychological wounds, but I did tell her that I was under Nazi occupation. She was undeterred and peppered me with questions. Faith was an important member of our synagogue and deeply connected to all things Jewish in Wilmington. She explained that the community held an annual commemoration of the Holocaust, and she encouraged me to share my experience and story.

"I cannot do it. I will cry and feel foolish."

Understanding the depth of my wounds she said, "Okay. Then tell me your story and I will relay it in your name."

I agreed. She wrote it out and returned to read it to me. It was all wrong. She said, "Then why don't you tell it and don't look at the audience; only look at me and you will be fine."

My first brief talk went well. The Jewish Community Center auditorium was full, and though I spoke for only 10 minutes, I did not cry. That was my measure of success. Afterward there were lots of questions and answers. I got immediate feedback and it was all positive. Another survivor, Dorothy Finger, introduced herself to me and said, "It was like hearing my own story." We later became friends. The Hebrew teachers in attendance all said, "You have to come and speak in our school!"

In the audience that evening was a teacher from St. Mary Magdalene School, a well-known Catholic school. She approached me and asked if I might speak to her students. She taught a Confraternity of Christian Doctrine (Catholic religious education) evening class. I explained the same thing to her. "I am afraid I will cry." She reassured me that crying is okay. That teacher, Barbara Rogers, remains my dear friend to this very day. In every school where Barbara Rogers taught, she invited me to speak to her class. She also introduced me to the Ulster Project that sends students from Northern Ireland to the United States to learn how to resolve conflicts peacefully. During the 1960s a civil rights movement began in Ulster raising awareness about the political and social rights of the Irish Catholic minority. This led to violence, pinning the Irish Republican Army (IRA) on the Catholic side against the Ulster Defense Force (UDF) on the Protestant side. Decades of Irish violence came to an end, but the scars inspired the Ulster project. These children, who were old enough to be influenced from an outside source, found meaning in my story.

I had adjusted to life in Delaware. I had new friends and started to teach part-time and volunteered whenever I could. Every second weekend I drove to Elizabeth, New Jersey, to spend time with my aging mother (who lived with my brother Joshua), and visit with the rest of my family.

Requests for me to speak came more frequently, primarily in schools and sometimes churches. Having been a teacher for some time, I learned to present my story so that students could understand what happened, why it happened, and how we could prevent similar catastrophes. If time would allow, I took questions from the audience.

A student once asked me, "Do you still hate all Germans?"

"Of course not," I said. It was that moment I realized that I must work into my presentation my father's teachings about the ugliness of hate, and how we can all become a force for good.

Thank you notes from students were reassuring and kind. They often contained expressions of gratitude for teaching them how to overcome hatred. The following is one example:

Dear Ms. Jaffe,

I just wanted to say thank you for taking the time out of your day to come and share your story with us. Your story was so inspiring, and I greatly admire your ability to keep hatred out of your mind after all that you endured at such an early age. You talked about how kindness, and hatred, are learned. I can only imagine how many kind people are out there because of you! Kindness is taught by example, and I fully intend to follow the one you have set. Words cannot express how grateful I am to have had the opportunity to listen to your story and learn from it.

Sincerely,

Lia

(the one kid that came up and asked if she could hug you.)

24

Chava

In 1980 my mother suffered a stroke and two years later she passed away peacefully in her own home with me standing at her side. The last word from her mouth was my name (Chana), as if to say, "I am glad you are here." She was 83 years old and my role model and true hero. Decades later when I was corresponding with my youngest brother, Sheldon, he wrote me back about our mother:

The Rambam says that the greatest creation that man can create is the refinement of his own personality. What a wonderful example we have of that in our own Mother. Born in[to] dire circumstances, (orphaned at the age of three) with no opportunity for education, she was thrown into the Nazi hell with 6 children to care for. Even now tears come to my eyes when I think [of] the suffering and humiliation she was forced to endure. Despite all of that, she was always a tower of strength to all of us, never losing her faith in mankind and always responding with love to all circumstances. She will always be a blessed memory to all her ever-increasing descendants.

As a college student, my son chose to write an essay about my mother:

David L. Jaffe
English 135
T, Th 1:30-3
Dr. Espey
September 24, 1985

BOBBY

My maternal grandmother's first and only conversational language was Yiddish, the tongue of pre-war Eastern European Jewry. My own knowledge of Yiddish is ridiculously informal; while I am familiar with hundreds of words, I cannot produce one grammatically correct sentence. Still, I understand everything my grandmother ever said to me. Perhaps I understood because of her intonation, emphasis or affect. Whatever the reason, I always knew what she meant. Her message was forever something about virtue, piety, or charity. She was endlessly giving something to someone else while never asking for anything in return. This was a woman who survived the horrors of the Holocaust, losing a son to the Nazis. Yet her faith in her Creator and in people never diminished.

Her courage helped save the lives of many during the war. Every now and then my mother will recall another incident where my grandmother's astuteness and bravery led to the survival of a few more people. Her common sense was evident even in her old age, as she gave sound logical advice to her daughter, my mother. Her name was Chava Swirsky, but we all just called her Bobby because the Yiddish word for grandmother is Bobeh and Bobby was just easier to say.

Coming to her house every Friday afternoon was a treat I and my sisters looked forward to during our child-

hood. Her kindness and love for her family gave her house a warm, comfortable glow that was all ours. Her Sabbath cooking smelled like a dream, and all of the children raced to the overburdened stove for a taste of the cholent, compote, bleen, or any one of a dozen other mouthwatering Jewish foods from Eastern Poland. I often wondered if my grandmother's house back in the tiny White Russian village of Kobylnik smelled the same way. In those days, the meal was cooked on a wood burning stove in a small-framed house located in a typical Jewish shtetl, not unlike Fiddler on the Roof's Anatevka. But the smell. . . the smell was the same. I pictured my mother and her siblings running to the large black pots just as I and my sisters did. I saw the same warm glow of love and reverence for the approaching Sabbath. I imaged my grandmother as a young woman, the spitting image of my mother today. I envisioned her standing over the mystical Sabbath candles, slowly, powerfully, waving her hands thrice in a circular motion, ushering in the Sabbath Queen just as she did so many times before my very eyes.

Now, thirty years later, she lived in America. During those thirty years she saw the very worst in Man, but she did not lose her faith in man. She had seen her cousins slaughtered, her neighbors shot, her son murdered. But she knew that to give up her faith or her courage was to hand Hitler a victory he came close to achieving. She would not succumb to the self-destructive trap of bitterness. Despite her personal tragedy, she tried to build a family imbued with the spirit of faith, tolerance, and sharing. She was always there to give a stranger a meal or a bed for the night, and she never called attention to the often laborious deeds of charity and self-sacrifice which she performed almost instinctively.

When she came to America, she worked for a living. She was employed by the orthodox community of Eliza-

beth, New Jersey to run the ritual Jewish immersion bath, or mikveh. Everyone knew Bobby as the Mikveh Lady. Women come to the mikveh for immersion after the menstrual period in order to symbolically cleanse their bodies of this impurity. I used to watch the women enter the building in their customary modest attire, and leave looking the same way. I wondered what effect the mikveh had on them. Were they spiritually cleansed? Was the spirit of the Lord in the water? What was Bobby's part in this ritual? I often walked into the mikveh building when no one was there. Inside was this large sunken bath, like a small swimming pool. Pink tiles covered its surface, and eight or nine steps led down to its full depth of about five feet. I treated it with respect because it held a certain mystical power which stirred me.

I never wondered if Bobby needed to use the mikveh. She seemed exempt to me. She was pious, she did not need such purification. I later realized how appropriate the job of running the mikveh was for Bobby. Her whole life was devoted to cleansing the spirit. The act of loving people and caring for them cleansed her daily. Each wrinkle on her old, beautiful face was not an age line but a purity line. She taught life's secrets to people who did not speak her language because her spirit's tongue was universal. She possessed the key to life, and I wondered how many people she touched with it.

My mother certainly felt her influence. Her love for Bobby was and is everlasting. When Bobby could no longer take care of herself, my mother was there for her, day in and day out for weeks at a time. When a stroke affected part of Bobby's face, making her words totally inaudible, my mother, as if by telepathy understood all. She stayed with Bobby until the last breath went out of my grandmother's delicate, battle-worn body. Such devotion is rare.

But is Bobby's spirit being diluted? After all, my mother does not go to the mikveh, and none of her children in our family were taught Yiddish, the beautiful but diminishing language. Are we failing her by not doing these things? Is our desire for material things affecting us? I hope not. I think we all have a part to play in promoting her goodness and understanding. It's just a different part. One which, I suppose, each of us has to find on our own.

Recalling the smell of Bobby's kitchen, I also remember another unique smell, not of food, but of her. It was a sweet, pruny scent which, during my grade school years, was only enjoyed when I threw my arms around her and kissed her soft drooping cheeks. On a recent trip home, something surprising yet comforting happened. After years of being without it, and almost forgetting it, that smell saturated my nostrils once again as I went to kiss my mother. At the same time, I noticed my mother's cheeks, with the same soft texture and just a hint of Bobby's droop. There she was, before my eyes. She was not one person but two-in-one. Perhaps she was three-in-one or a hundred-in-one. I know nothing of my great-grandmother or any other ancestors. But maybe I do. Maybe they all live in my mother and someday will live in me. I don't know. What I do know is that I'm going home more often now.

* * *

Mother asked to be buried in Israel next to her husband, and my brother Joshua took care of all the arrangements which included exhuming Father's remains in Canada and having them delivered, with Mother to Israel. Their internment together in Israel was the end of a most remarkable love story.

We were still mourning my mother's passing when we learned that my sister Mina was sick with an aggressive form of leukemia. I adored my only sister, and we were all devastated with this news. Her prognosis was not good, but the experts all tried to give us some hope. If we could prolong her life, science might find a cure. I tried to spend as much time as I could with her in New York at the Sloan Kettering hospital and at home. I didn't want to leave her side, but my daughter Linda—who had moved to Israel after college—was getting married there and Mina told me, "Go." Two years after her diagnosis she passed away at the age of 51, while I was at tending Linda's wedding.

25

A Speaking Career

From 1977 when Faith Brown first coaxed me into sharing publicly a bit of my story, and Barbara Rogers kept inviting me back to speak to her students, I finally realized the effect it had on the listeners. I knew that there was no stopping. I understood that most older Holocaust survivors did not have the communication skills to handle large crowds. So, I felt that I must do everything I could to share and educate, especially about the destructive nature of discrimination and hatred. The response from the students was overwhelming. All in all, for almost 40 years, I was invited back to hundreds of classrooms, churches, community centers, and study groups. Other teachers felt that the subsequent classes each year must also learn this lesson. For that reason, I was invited back year after year and made strong friendships with those teachers.

At times there were moments of real disruption by unhappy students. My teaching skills helped me deal with every unique situation. My goal was clear; I was there to share my story and try to teach these young people history, and the lessons of my father, "We must care for everyone regardless of religion, race, or political party." By just being kind and understanding to those who didn't want to be at an assembly, the disruptions almost always disappeared, and the message was received.

Centerville Layton School, Wilmington, DE

2/21/2020

Dear Mrs. Jaffe,

Thank you for taking time to visit our school. Your speech and presentation of your experiences was truly moving. I learned how and why to love and forgive, even in times of great suffering. What was done to you and your family was absolutely despicable and unforgivable. Yet somehow, you managed to let go of all of your anger and hate, and that is one of the many valuable lessons to be learned from your life story. What was truly inspiring was the fact that you learned, and now teach, to love your enemy. You also may end up saving someone if you act out of the pure kindness of your heart, no matter how small the deed. Your bravery, courage, and pure resilience is a marvel, and what you have taught us will most certainly be passed on through countless generations. You will never be forgotten. Thank you.

Sincerely,

Evan Koller (Teacher)

In 2001 there was a local initiative called "Why Remember?" It was co-sponsored by the United States Holocaust Memorial Museum, our local newspaper (*The News Journal*) and the largest bank conglomerate in Wilmington, Delaware at that time (MBNA). I was invited to speak at the largest theater in town, The DuPont Playhouse. There were over 1,000 students from all surrounding areas.

Students were quoted in the newspaper the following day saying, "Amazing . . . but horrible too. I was trying not to cry." (Jane MacCaroon, 12 years old). "[I had learned a little about the Holocaust], but nothing like this. [She has] changed the way I look at life." (Maria Alvarez, 13).

Shortly thereafter, *The News Journal* reporter contacted me to arrange another large address, this time at the University of Delaware campus at the Bob Carpenter Center, which is their sports arena. For that address, Delaware high school students were bused in from all over. This time there were more than 1,000 students present. That was the largest address I ever gave.

I also spoke in neighboring states. Downingtown, PA had an annual program teaching the Holocaust to the tenth graders. Many survivors were invited (primarily from Philadelphia). I was also invited to participate in that program which spawned a great friendship with many students and teachers. One of those students created a book for her class project and named it *A Promise Kept*. I returned many times.

I never turned down an invitation to speak unless I was unwell. There were school semesters when I spoke two or three times a week. As you might imagine, throughout the years I was invited to very diverse groups and locations including a visit to the Delaware Women's Prison, when a prisoner told me, "If you can overcome hatred and all the things that happened to you, I know that I will be able to overcome my incarceration." I was also invited to a Delaware airbase and spoke to a group of pilots and engineers. They gave me a plaque in the shape of a fighter jet wing in gratitude of my service.

In 2010 I received a phone call from a former student of mine. She had moved to Mississippi when she married and now was a mother of two herself. Active in the local PTA she learned that her daughter's history class was learning about WWII and was hoping to have a Holocaust survivor speak. She thought of me and wasted no time in calling and making the request.

"We will cover all of your expenses for travel if you agree."

I had spoken in states near Delaware but had never flown to a southern state to speak and it felt like a wonderful opportunity. However, I was not confident enough to travel alone so I counter offered.

"I will come if you allow me to bring a chaperone."

"Done," she said.

My daughter, Linda—who had returned with her family to the United States in 1992—agreed to take a few days off from her work to come with me.

We flew to Meridian, Mississippi, and were picked up at the airport and briefed on the schedule. For one overnight, I spoke three times!

The first was in a public school that was predominantly African American. People were extremely kind, and when we arrived at the school we were met with reporters and ushered quickly into an area designated for the speaker before entering the school auditorium. In that very large auditorium, we were met with about 900 guests, most of them from the student body. Almost every seat was taken, and the atmosphere was electric. I thought to myself that most of these young people probably know very little about people like me and the Holocaust. I was fulfilling my mission. Among those present was a local businessman named Bruce Martin who had heard about my talk. He would soon play an interesting role in my return to Mississippi.

As usual I spoke for approximately one hour and then took a few questions. My daughter, Linda, sat in the front row taking notes. She told me she was absolutely struck by how such a very large group of teenage students was so quiet. Every student in that auditorium was listening intently to what I had to share. When it was all over and the students were dismissed, a long line of people formed to meet me down in front of the stage. Many wanted my photograph, but one girl of Indian heritage asked whether she could touch my feet.

I giggled at the notion, and said "Sure, but why?"

She said, "In my culture, this is how we show our respect."

So, I replied, "Of course." She knelt and touched my shoes. My daughter Linda speaks of this scene often because it was unlike any other acknowledgement I had ever had.

That same evening, I spoke at a community college in Meridian. It had been advertised but the group was relatively small, approximately 50 disparate adults. The following morning, before our return flight, I was to speak at a private school in Meridian, which was entirely Caucasian. This was the class of my former student's daughter. The group was smaller than 50 students. They were respectful but had little interest in asking questions.

Julie and Bruce Martin swung into action. After hearing my talk at the public school, they were convinced I must come back to speak to their religious community. They called and repeated the offer to cover all our expenses. Linda joined me again. We returned to Meridian about a year later and I spoke to a packed church with standing room only in the rear. It was the same message, but among a crowd like this the post talk Q&A was different. One man stood up and asked a politically charged question of why his cultural group was not being treated fairly, and the crowd was visibly upset. I handled the question by saying that I do not get involved in politics.

Immediately following the church talk we were invited to a reception in my honor. Greg Cartmell, a local artist, approached Linda and said, "I like to paint portraits, especially of people who make a difference in this world. I would like to paint your mother."

Linda fumbled with how we could afford or even make this happen, when Greg explained, "I am giving the portrait to her as a gift and can paint it from a photograph."

Naturally we agreed, and Linda sent the photo with my consent and corresponded with Greg for several months. Approximately one year later we received a large and lovely oil portrait.

Before the portrait was in our hands, a third invitation followed. Bruce Martin wanted me to speak at his alma mater, Mississippi State University. Linda and I traveled to Starksville, Mississippi, and were received by the faculty and Dean with great enthusiasm. This talk was very well advertised. I was exhausted from the travel and needed to rest beforehand, but a small campus Hillel group wanted to meet with me beforehand. I asked Linda to meet with them instead, and it was a good plan. Linda had a unique experience, and I got much needed rest before the big lecture.

The main talk was held that evening in a large lecture hall that held approximately 300 seats. The auditorium quickly filled up. In order to accommodate almost double that amount of people who had already arrived, an extra room was promptly arranged. The Dean delayed the start of the lecture to arrange for 500 more people, who sat audience style in the overflow room, to watch the lecture in real time on closed-circuit TV. That event was recorded and can still be viewed online at:

http://vimeo.com/30390185.

Now, when people are interested in what I used to teach, I point them to this video.

26

Returning to My Past

After the Soviet Union fell apart in the early 1990s our eldest brother Meyer, who still lived in Israel, immediately traveled to our old hometown to see what remained. The name of the town had changed from Kobylnik to Naroch, and the population of the town was transformed from 1,200 people to approximately 8,000. Meyer was terribly disappointed that there was hardly a sign left of the mass grave where the last 120 Jews were killed by the Nazis. The only way he recognized the place was by visible human remains. We understood that some of the local drunks who were trying to look for gold teeth or some money that the victims might have had on them, opened that grave and extracted from it whatever they could. They did not bother to rebury the bones. My brother arranged for a grave marker and fence around the site. When he returned to Israel, he told us that it was safe to travel now.

The next trip in 1994 was my first time back since we left Europe. I was accompanied by my brother Joshua, and a few other survivors from Kobylnik. Our first mission was to find the people who were kind to us and helped us during the war years. On one such expedition, we went to the village where my father was recognized by his voice only, and that farmer did not let him go begging anymore, providing food from the community. We found that village almost totally empty. There was hardly a human in sight. All the young people left for the bigger cities. Only a few older people were left behind.

Walking around we noticed a very old woman and as we approached her, she asked us, "What are you looking for?"

When we told her the name of the kind farmer, she told us "Oh, he died many years ago. One of his sons still lives here in the village. He must be somewhere in the fields collecting hay for the winter. If you go out to the fields, you will probably find him."

There were a few other farmers collecting hay for their animals for the winter. One of them directed us to the man we were looking for. I cannot remember his name anymore. When we finally got to talk to this old man, he was shocked to realize that we remembered his father from the war years. We told him that we wanted to express our gratitude for his father's kindness and my brother and I each gave him a $100 bill. He was awe struck, because to him $200 was a fortune. We couldn't resist taking a picture with him so that our children will remember the farmer and our journey back to thank his son.

It was during this visit that we unveiled the stone monument at the site of the mass grave. Meyer had it sent from a larger city, and it included a metal plaque engraved with the names of those massacred. Below their names, a message was permanently fixed to the area in the local language:

If you are passing by this place, stop and meditate. This is a sacred place where the Nazis killed 120 innocent Jewish victims.

The fence built around the grounds was substantial, with a stone base and wrought iron top in the shape of Jewish stars.

The whole village was invited to come to our dedication of the mass grave, including the town priest and the current Mayor. I remember Meyer's speech was so moving that I could not stop crying. He begged the village people to take care of this place: "The victims who were buried here were innocent people, your farmer's neighbors." The priest, who was a young man and new to the community, did not have much to add. Some of the elderly women spoke up and said that they remembered the executions. These old women were youngsters then and had joined their mothers to witness the executions. They still remember the Jewish mothers begging them to take their children. They explained, "We were scared."

It was during this first trip back that I reunited with my childhood friend, Maya. During a visit to Postavy, where we were visiting a Jewish family that we knew, I told the older woman I was looking for Maya. I explained rumors that Maya had moved to Leningrad, now St. Petersburg, and needed someone who could help me find her.

The woman told me, "She is back here, already for a long time. She lives close by. Let me call her."

In 30 minutes, she arrived at the house. I didn't recognize her after more than 50 years. Her hair was an orange-red and it seemed to me that she had grown. But as soon as we started talking, we fell into each other's arms and enjoyed the warmest of embraces. We could not stop talking to one another. I returned to see Maya during each subsequent trip back to Belarus. I also sent her a ticket to Wilmington, Delaware to spend a month with us. Years later her daughter called me to let me know that Maya had died of Alzheimer's. She was cremated. I still think about her often.

In 2004 I made my second trip back to Belarus with my daughter Rebecca and my son David. We had decided only one month earlier to take the trip and Linda could not get away from work at that time. My brothers, Meyer and Joshua, joined us and they were a tremendous help. Meyer ordered a van and took us all around. One highlight was visiting the Partisan Museum located in the forest. Another was to be a part of the anniversary programs. It was very meaningful for all of us to be together in this place.

I made several other trips back. I had prearranged a visit to Belarus, when Rebecca and her family decided to first meet me in the old country on the way to their trip to Israel. Their visit was short, but this gave her children and husband the opportunity to experience my living history. I returned home, and they continued to Israel and celebrated my grandson's bar mitzvah at the Western Wall in Jerusalem.

My husband, Ed, now wanted to go back to his hometown and once again we traveled to Europe. Although our hometowns were approximately 20 kilometers apart, Adutishki fell into the newer drawn country lines of Lithuania, while Naroch was in Belarus. We stayed in Vilna, where hotels were more comfortable, but ultimately found a driver to take us to Adutishki and we found a very old woman who still remembered his family.

27

Legislative Change

At 91 years old I remain the last survivor to speak regularly in Wilmington. I have been honored in my community many times (Israeli Bonds, Hadassah, and Delaware Women's Hall of Fame). I was also chosen as an honoree by the Anti-Defamation League (ADL). I am humbled by every acknowledgement of what I have done. But nothing compares to the last achievement.

I joined the Holocaust Education Committee in Wilmington, Delaware, when it was first established in the late 1970s. Our main goal was to persuade the Delaware legislature to institute Holocaust Education in the Delaware school system. Unfortunately, they resisted our efforts. In 2019, Steve Gonzer, our committee leader, called me to say that we now had an invitation to the state capital, in Dover (June 2019), to plead our case before the Delaware legislature for mandated Holocaust Education. I was not sure what my role would be, but Steve said as a survivor I needed to go and explain my perspective. I was reluctant because I had never spoken to lawmakers before. I prepared these words for the address:

My name is Ann Jaffe. I am a Holocaust survivor. In 1975 my late husband, Edward Jaffe, who was a chemist with the DuPont company was transferred to Wilmington, Delaware. The past 45 years have been the best years of my life.

I am a retired teacher of Judaic Studies who has made it my life's mission to educate as many young students as possible about the horrors of WWII. I never refuse an invitation from any school, college, or church to share my personal experience of that period and the lessons that we can learn from it. To date, I have spoken over 450 times.

I am the youngest of all the survivors here in Delaware and I am almost 89 years old.

Yesterday was the 75th International Holocaust Remembrance Day. How can people remember something they have never known or witnessed?

In written history 75 years is practically current events. And yet when I speak to hundreds of students in both private and public schools many of them know few details regarding the Holocaust.

There have been other horrific genocides in history—which we also need to learn and understand, but the Holocaust was a state-sponsored, calculated, and systematic killing of millions of innocent people, among whom were six-million documented Jews.

As legislators, perhaps ask yourself whether this was taught to you in school? Just as importantly, as it is my obligation to remember, we must teach that if this can happen once, it can happen again.

Education is the first step and I commend you all for elevating the state of Delaware by joining eleven other states that require Holocaust education in schools.

*When I am gone, I want to make sure that future gen-
erations of students will learn the history of that period.
We must acknowledge that it happened; we must teach our
children the facts; and we must help them process those facts
in a personal way so they realize this could have been their
race, their religion, or their culture. That is what it was—a
tragic world event that targeted completely innocent people
because an insane dictator came to power, while others went
along with him, and others looked the other way too long.*

*Not only will this help us raise better people and a better
world, but it will also help Americans better appreciate the
freedom that we enjoy in the United States of America.
Thank you.*

Both the Delaware House of Representatives and
the State Senate unanimously passed the Bill, and it was
subsequently signed into law. In 2020, the Halina Wind
Preston Holocaust Committee, under the guidance and
leadership of Steve Gonzer, worked with local legislatures to
finally enact a law in Delaware mandating that the Holocaust
be taught in public schools. Delaware became the 13th state
to do so, and I was present on a Zoom call when the bill
was signed by our Governor, John Carney. Our Holocaust
Education Committee is currently working to guide public
school teachers on the best way to introduce this material
to young people. I am gratified that our mission was
accomplished.

Also, in 2020, a world pandemic struck: Coronavirus, better known as COVID-19. Schools went virtual and that was
the last time I spoke to a crowd in person. I am still speaking,
but to individuals who will pass along these lessons.

My daughter Linda has commented that she sees I cannot read enough written material about the war years.

"Why do you keep immersing yourself in something so
difficult?" she asks.

It is a good question. When you have been through this horror, and have only your specific experience in hand, both my brother and I want to learn and hear every fact we can to understand better the full picture. It is also why I find myself drawn to other survivors and now will go out of my way to speak regularly to anyone I know who is still alive.

For example, just days ago I was watching TV and happened upon an interview of a new author, Adam P. Frankel, who wrote *The Survivors*. It turns out that his grandfather was someone we knew! I called and spoke to Adam's mother. I suppose we feel that nobody can fully understand what it was like unless you were actually there, and that is why we crave to share our stories with those that have suffered the same.

As an answer to my daughter: my past is part of my everyday life to this day. The family I was privileged to have means so very much to me. Which brings me to my own children.

With exceptional intellect and motivation, Rebecca graduated a year early from high school and went directly to a six-year medical program, becoming a Doctor of Medicine just before her 23rd birthday. Rebecca decided to do her residency in Wilmington. This was a gift to me, as I had hoped to have my children close by. We were so proud of her and overjoyed that she chose to reside close to the family. It did not take Rebecca long to open a private practice which flourished for 30 years. Currently she is working at a start-up company that is helping reshape family medicine. Her career has been amazing. It was Rebecca's musicality and artistic ability that strongly influenced Linda.

Linda attended the University of Delaware. She was passionate about theater and participated in all her high school and college productions. This is not what we had in mind when we sent her for ballet lessons as a child, but it made her happy. Shortly after her first year in college I noticed a lump in her neck. She was diagnosed with Hodgkin's Lymphoma. I found an excellent doctor at the University of Pennsylvania who agreed to treat her and reassured me that she would be okay. Once she was past her treatments, she made up for lost time and graduated with a degree in Business Administration. She was not sure of her next step.

My brother Meyer who lived in Israel happened to be visiting us in the States at that time and suggested that Linda come to Israel for a year. She quickly jumped at the idea, and with trepidation, but also our blessing, she departed for Israel, knowing that Meyer would look after her. Best of all, this gave me the perfect reason to visit Israel every year and see both of my brothers! All my brothers were a source of great inspiration in my life, and Linda lived in Israel for nine years where my first two grandchildren were born. Ultimately, Linda worked as a long term Judicial Assistant for the United States Court of Appeals, enjoying a career with an exceptional Judge and dozens of aspiring young lawyers.

David loved sports. In school he tried everything but ultimately played baseball, ran track and field, and even participated in gymnastics. Above all he excelled in debating and student government. David finished high school with honors and went to the University of Pennsylvania. He was not far from home, but this did make us empty nesters. He went on to Harvard Medical School, also becoming a physician, and received a Fellowship in Boston remaining there for several years. With Linda in Israel and David in Boston, two of my children were far away. After Boston David moved a little closer, living and working in New York City for approximately ten years. Ultimately, he was able to get a Professorship closer to us at the Hospital of the University of Pennsylvania, where he continues to work to this day.

Our first Delaware home, which we bought hastily in 1975, needed a great deal of work and repair. Ed was working long hours and traveling a lot. When I suggested to him that it would be easier to just move to a new house rather than fix the current one, he agreed. I found a quiet cul-de-sac where new homes were being built. We signed a contract while they were still being constructed so we were able to design the interior to our liking. We moved into that new house in January of 1992. It was a big house for two people, but I loved to entertain and had large groups of friends over often, especially for the holidays.

Eight months after moving to our new home Linda and her family moved back to Wilmington from Israel. Her marriage was suffering, and the 1991 Gulf War impacted her already compromised health. She wanted the comfort of her family. I was thrilled. Her two daughters, then six and three years old, were adorable and brought us great joy. Though I was still teaching part-time, I spent as much time as possible with them, especially after Linda and her husband started working full-time. Ultimately, Linda divorced years later.

Rebecca married and gave me two more wonderful grandchildren, whom I adore. As the need has arisen in my old age, Rebecca, and her generous husband, Jerome Heisler, Jr. have taken over much of the family hosting. We all benefit from Jerry's talent for cooking. Now all my direct descendants live within a reasonable car drive from me, which allows us to see each other often. It is my greatest joy.

* * *

As I reflect back, I had a good and satisfying life. My first ten years in the village house where I was born, though modest, seemed like the best place in the world because of the people that lived and loved there. I was blessed with a wonderful grandmother and exceptional parents, who taught me the importance of a tight-knit family.

The next three years under Nazi occupation were hell on earth. We were all starving, and I was afraid night and day, not only for my life, but also for the lives of my siblings and parents. It was so cruel that there were many times I remember thinking that death would be better.

After liberation, two years in Russia taught my father about Communism. He got our family out of there as soon as possible. Displaced Persons Camps housed us the next five years. It was during these years I matured and became a young woman. Most importantly, it was at this time I learned a life-changing lesson from my father, about the destructive nature of hate. I share his wisdom at every opportunity and with every public address.

We were glad to leave Europe behind us and start a new life on the American continent. For three years in Canada, I immersed myself in the study of English. I also worked full time to help support our family. After my marriage, I moved to the United States of America. I am forever grateful to this country that allowed us to build a new life. The first three years in the States I worked to support my husband who was completing his PhD in Chemistry.

As a new mother my focus was on giving my children every advantage and opportunity. I know my family is in good hands all around. Each of them possesses and employs the lessons of my father: Never hate. Be an example for others. Be kind and respectful.

Now that you have read my story, you are also a surrogate survivor. Tell this story to anyone who will listen. Ask them, in kind, to share this story and the lessons of hatred, and encourage tolerance for our few differences, but to focus on how much we are all fundamentally alike.

Touch everyone you know with kindness.

* * *

April 28, 2013

Dear Ann,

Yours is a life well lived.

While I was tucked in at night under a warm blanket, you were almost freezing in a forest. When I didn't want to finish my dinner, you didn't have any dinner. You witnessed unspeakable atrocities that I cannot even imagine. Yet you came out of a horrific situation, that was not of your own choosing, as a forward looking, optimistic, charitable compassionate person.

I so admire what you are doing to make people understand what happened to you during the Holocaust. When one talks about six million people, it doesn't have nearly the impact as when one talks about one person or one family. Big numbers numb the mind—people can relate to you as you tell your personal story. Perhaps by doing what you do, you will make unthinking people think. Surely, there will be fewer people who can deny the Holocaust.

I wish you many more years to tell your story.

Rischa Fishman

Acknowledgements

This story would never have been written if it were not for my daughter Linda's support, patience, and efforts. My dear friend Diane Isaacs who cheered me on and gently helped me push through the entire process; as well as David and Rebecca who helped everyone and encouraged and participated in the completion of the project. A special thank you to my brother, Yehoshua (Joshua) who, for decades, spent weekends with me continually talking and reminding me about the old days and of the names of a few people and places I had lost to time.

My gratitude extends to all the teachers and their employers, with whom I developed ongoing relationships and continued to invite me back to speak with their students, year after year. Equally so, thank you to all those students who agreed to share my story with their parents and friends.

Thank you to Sheryl Davidson, who invited me to Mississippi to speak with three groups. Additional gratitude to Julie and Bruce Martin for inviting me back to Mississippi two more times. Thank you to Mississippi State University for hosting me and joining other institutions to later post my talk online for all to experience. And thank you to Gregory Cartmell who painted my portrait with no remuneration.

I am grateful to the Halina Wind Preston Holocaust Education Committee (in Delaware) and Regina Alonzo who worked hard to keep the committee going for so many years. Extra gratitude to my friend, Steve Gonzer (who took over after Regina), and who was the driving force behind the legislative action to make teaching the Holocaust mandatory in public schools in Delaware. His ongoing contributions are hard to quantify. He is a mensch of the highest order.

Finally, to Jaidy Schweers, whose bright spirit and professionalism brought this project to fruition.

Ann Jaffe, 2021

Additional Stories
about Mother's Family

I have tremendously fond memories of my maternal grandmother Rivka, who was a striking and beautiful woman. She was tall and sturdy, with dark wavy hair, which she always had pulled back in a low braid, pinned at her neck. While in her early 30's she was widowed with four children. Rivka could have easily remarried because of her age and beauty, but she was overheard saying, "I cannot imagine any other man being the father to my children." Men noticed her through the years, but she never let on to have a notion of beginning again with another man. She seemed immovable in that regard. She decided to raise her children alone and remained single the rest of her life.

It took close to a year for her to fully recover from the shock of losing her husband, but she knew she had to pick up and carry on much sooner than that. She wasn't sure how she would make a living, but a town friend took her aside and said, "Rivka, you must raise your children. You cannot live on the dole of the town. You have to learn to do something!" Throwing around a few ideas, together they decided what she would do. That same friend taught her how to bake bagels and specialty rolls. She baked those fresh "bagelach" weekly, so that on the designated town market day she would go out and sell enough bread to support them through the week. Her town nickname was, "Rivka the Bekkerke," (Rivka the Baker), and she was one of many stoic, independent and courageous women in a small town at that time in history. Her baking vocation allowed Rivka to live with dignity. Later in life, she was a pseudo mother to her grandchildren that included me. She disciplined us, took us out to the nearby forest to learn about edible flowers and mushrooms, and simply loved and cared for us when mother was working. She was truly loved, and I named my first daughter after her.

Besides my mother, Rivka had three other children. Mother's oldest brother, Yesheya, also survived the war, although Yesheya's wife and three daughters were taken away and killed. His three sons survived. Rivka's second born was Yossel (Joseph), who emigrated to the United States just before the war took hold. The third child was a girl, Slava. Mother was the fourth born. The fifth baby was born after my grandfather died, and we think probably died from neglect, as Rivka was in shock and could barely manage the four small children she had at the time.

Yesheya was an unusually striking man with a broad chest, and a head of thick curly black hair. As the oldest son, he was drafted into the Russian army early and came back an even more robust man, over whom the young girls in our town often ogled. Because our homes didn't have bathrooms, he went out to the well without his shirt to wash up. All eyes were on him as he displayed a striking figure. I think he knew they were watching him.

A distant cousin of mine fell head-over-heels in love with Yesheya. She had found a way to travel to the states (well before the war) and worked in the garment district in New York City saving her meager wages to send home a ticket, so that Yesheya might come and marry her. Like a dowry, in those days, a ticket to the new country could persuade a man to marry. Our cousin dreamt of a chance to marry Yesheya and worked extremely hard to send him the funds. When she got word he was on the way, she found out his arrival date, watched for notification, and set time aside to go down to the docks to meet him at the vessel. One can only imagine how excited she was, having set all her energy and hopes on his hand in marriage. As the voyagers disembarked, she almost fainted to see that Yossel, Yesheya's younger brother, had arrived in his place.

When the money for the ticket had arrived back home, Yossel (the second son born to Rivka) was being called up to the Russian army. The family feared for Yossel, as his image and stature were quite different than Yesheya. Yossel was gentle and less attractive, and they knew that the Russians would make his life miserable, first and foremost because he was a Jew, but even more so because he was meek. Feeling they had no choice, they gave Yossel the ticket so that he could escape the army. Our cousin (in New York) could not be consoled.

The only aunt I really knew was Rivka's third child, Slava, who finally did marry, and moved with her husband to Vilna, the closest big city. I can still remember visiting her there before the war. She had two sons, and their entire family was killed along with other Vilna Jews in Panary (a place designated for mass executions by the Nazis).

Yesheya did not come with us when we left Europe. He decided to stay in Russia and died a relatively young man in 1956. Years later we got word of his startling death.

Yesheya's oldest son, Yisroel Leib, had been drafted into the Russian army. Having suffered the loss of his wife and three daughters, Yesheya remained in Europe so that his son would not return from the army to an empty home. Hertzke and Irwin stayed with our family for many years. Ultimately, Hertzke went to Palestine (now Israel) and Irwin (who had been called Itzke) went to Canada and remained my close friend until his death. He had been like a brother to me as we were the same age and lived in the same house for many years.

Years passed and Yisroel Leib returned to ultimately marry and have a child of his own. A few years later Yesheya was hospitalized for what we presumed was pneumonia and was in the hospital looking out the window when he saw a Jewish funeral procession. His interest was natural, because with so few Jews left in the area, he thought he must know the person being buried. Jewish law requires that a person usually be buried the next day, barring exceptional circumstance. Yesheya asked a nurse about the deceased. Hospital staff returned to explain, "It is your son Yisroel Leib who died of a sudden heart attack." The shock of this utterly devastating news caused Yesheya to collapse from what we suspect was a heart attack. He died the same day as his son, in the hospital where he was being treated.

Additional Stories
about Father's Family

My father came from a family of educated men. Both his grandfather and great-grandfather were clergy. This is probably why they were not as well off as other Jewish families that were merchants. *Scholars don't bring home money, they study.* Both sides of his family had little income. His grandmother was the only one who worked and made their living. The other side of the "scholar" coin was that educated people were well respected and would often expect to marry a woman who came from a wealthier family. That was also the case for my father, but we already know what happened with him. He waited ten years to marry a poor girl, because he was convinced that she was the right person for him.

Both my grandmothers were very independent women who provided all the income for their families. Although I was raised in a society largely driven by men, this is partially why I believe in a woman's ability to be strong and resourceful.

My father had a couple of siblings who died very young. I know very little about them, except that they were artistic people. Among the siblings that survived was one brother that emigrated to the United States. He was my Uncle Herman (*Chaim* in Yiddish). My father also had two sisters who perished in the Holocaust; the older one lived in the neighboring town, and the younger one had married shortly before the war and had a baby. They were among the first to be killed.

Although we didn't have as close a relationship with my father's mother, we did see her often and showed her due respect. She had a difficult temperament and was a very strict individual; when we came to her house there was a lot of "don't touch that," and "you cannot touch that either!" We were required to behave a certain way, and it made us fidgety. She lived in the same town, and every Shabbos, after we ate, there was an obligatory visit to Grandmother.

My mother's life was made tougher because of her mother-in-law. You see, Father's mother was not only a hypochondriac, but she had two younger daughters (my aunts on Father's side), both of whom constantly needed help with things. One never married, and the other did, but to a poor man. So, Father was constantly being called upon to help physically and financially with everything associated with them. This was something my mother had to put up with on a regular basis. The temperament of her mother-in-law only added to the trouble.

Because Father's moneymaking endeavors weren't always successful at bringing in enough for our own family, it turned out that my mother was the primary caregiver of both our family and Father's core family. We never heard her complain about it. She realized this was her duty and she met it with dignity and respect. She was remarkable in almost every way.

My father's mother died in 1938, when I was only seven years old. I remember what she looked like and going to her house. She regularly insisted that Father take her to the doctor (which was costly), because she thought she had heart problems. I remember resenting this, but in the end, I do think she died of a heart attack, but I have never been sure.

Ann Jaffe Honors

Philadelphia Hadassah Israeli Bonds (2007)
Wilmington Hadassah Lifetime Achievement
Anti-Defamation League Honoree People Against Hate (2016)
Hadassah's Woman of the Year (2017)
Delaware Women's Hall of Fame (2020)

Lightning Source UK Ltd.
Milton Keynes UK
UKHW040753041222
413249UK00005B/879